Waxing On

Waxing On

THE KARATE KID AND ME

Ralph Macchio

DUTTON

DUTTON

An imprint of Penguin Random House LLC
penguinrandomhouse.com

Copyright © 2022 by Ralph Macchio

YOU'RE THE BEST (from *The Karate Kid*)
Words and Music ALLEE WILLIS and BILL CONTI
© 1985 EMI GOLDEN TORCH MUSIC CORP. and EMI APRIL MUSIC INC.
All Rights Administered by SONY MUSIC PUBLISHING
Exclusive Print Right for EMI GOLDEN TORCH MUSIC CORP.
Controlled and Administered by ALFRED MUSIC
All Rights Reserved
Used by Permission of ALFRED MUSIC

You're The Best
Words and Music by Allee Willis and Bill Conti
Copyright © 1984 EMI April Music Inc. and EMI Golden Torch Music Corp.
All Rights on behalf of EMI April Music Inc.
Administered by Sony Music Publishing (US) LLC,
424 Church Street, Suite 1200, Nashville, TN 37219
International Copyright Secured All Rights Reserved
Reprinted by Permission of Hal Leonard LLC

LIBRARY OF CONGRESS CATALOGING-IN-PUBLICATION DATA
has been applied for.

ISBN 9780593185834 (hardcover)
ISBN 9780593185841 (ebook)

Printed in the United States of America
1st Printing

BOOK DESIGN BY KRISTIN DEL ROSARIO

In memory of
John G. Avildsen
and Noriyuki "Pat" Morita

. . . the **honor**

To Phyllis, Julia, and Daniel

. . . the **balance**

CONTENTS

———

CONTENTS

Waxing On

INTRODUCTION

T he movie's release date was set.

June 22, 1984.

The calendar page had flipped past the middle of May, and by that point I had not seen a frame of the finished product—only limited pieces of a black-and-white work print a few months earlier, when I was called in to participate in post-production sound. I had been getting word that the "advance tracking was very good." However, I had heard those types of phrases before, and most often they would lead to an underwhelming result. But in this case, what was about to happen to me was different. What would play out in front of me on a spring evening in New York City turned out to be, well . . . magic.

On May 19, 1984, at seven P.M., a sneak preview of Columbia Pictures' *The Karate Kid* was happening in 1,100 theaters around the country. I'd be at the Baronet and Coronet Theatre on Third Avenue in Manhattan. There I would see the completed film for the first time, with a public audience. No private screening scenario with jaded executives and talent reps. This was a Saturday Evening Picture Show for paying customers. There was a long line of "regular people" of all ages stretching down Third and around the corner onto Fifty-Ninth Street.

As the audience filed into the theater, my girlfriend (now wife of thirty-five years) and I met up with the film's director, John G. Avildsen (an Oscar winner for *Rocky*); its brilliant screenwriter, Robert Mark Kamen; and legendary film producer Jerry Weintraub. We sat in the last row of the packed auditorium. I slipped in fairly unnoticed except for a few random audience members who waved to me and referenced Francis Ford Coppola's *The Outsiders,* the film I had appeared in a year prior. Other than that, I was pretty civilian in an audience of real people. I was quite nervous and a bit skeptical but ultimately eager in anticipation of what lay ahead.

The lights went down. The audience began to quiet and settle. The butterflies increased in my stomach as Bill Conti's sweeping music underscored the opening credits. On the screen, this "Karate Kid" took that green station-wagon ride with his widowed mom from Newark, New Jersey, to Reseda, California.

The movie was only a few minutes in when they arrived at the South Seas Apartments in the San Fernando Valley. However, it seemed like somehow everyone in that audience already had an understanding or some connection with this kid, this Daniel LaRusso. They related to this kid, they liked this kid, they laughed with him, they hurt with him, and ultimately, they cheered for him.

As this underdog story unfolded on the screen in front of me, the love affair with the theater's audience seemed to build and heighten with each and every frame. Every laugh. Every ooh and aah. Every punch. Every kick. Every tear. Every cheer . . . it was all in concert. Four hundred people seemingly sharing one brain in one collective experience in the life of this kid . . . and this kid . . . was me. Holy crap. I mean, yeah, I was twenty-two years old at the time and LaRusso was only turning sixteen—more on that "yoot-ful" appearance later (a cheap *My Cousin Vinny* reference, sure, but I was in that one too, and after all, this is my story).

Now, I'm not saying that this feeling was unprecedented. There have been many film audiences, before and after, that I am sure have shared the same connection with a lead character. But from my point of view, in the humblest way—I mean, come on, I was just the Long Island guy who got the part— this was surreal. I had been in a few things, an ensemble TV series and a very cool Coppola film, but this was something else. I was in virtually every frame of this thing, and the response was extraordinary. Daniel LaRusso was being lifted to heroic proportions, and it was like nothing I had ever experienced before. The Baronet Theatre was electric, and I was on the ride of a lifetime.

I have often described sitting in the back of that theater as like being in the back of the coolest roller coaster, witnessing everyone's heads, shoulders, and arms moving in unison as the track took them on different turns, drops, and ascents.

The movie's themes of bullying and mentorship connected on all cylinders. It was genuine wish fulfillment, as every setup was paying off to perfection. We followed a bullied teenager under the soulful tutelage of his martial arts master, a surrogate father figure and virtual human Yoda, Mr. Miyagi—portrayed in a brilliant, Oscar-nominated performance by my friend and screen partner the late, great Noriyuki "Pat" Morita. Miyagi's unorthodox training techniques played out as a beautiful cinematic magic trick. Daniel LaRusso was the every-kid next door who had no business winning anything and a classic aspirational character who was overcoming the odds, heading toward the ultimate climax, where he represented a piece of all of us.

There, at the All Valley Karate Championship, against the villainous Cobra Kai, I would hear the now famous "Sweep the leg" and "Get him a body bag" (who knew?) for the first time as the anticipation of the crane kick loomed around the corner.

The swell of excitement was palpable. Conti's music built. Avildsen's edits elevated. LaRusso assumes the position. I could feel the dam about to burst. And then . . . the kick! The crescendo! Boom! A thunderous roar from the Baronet Theatre crowd as they leapt to their feet, cheering and hugging and high-fiving as if at a major-league sporting event. It was a thrilling rush of emotion and I was sucked into the vortex like I had just won the World Series, Super Bowl, and Stanley Cup at the same time! I don't think I even remember the credits rolling.

This continued up the aisles of the theater, through the lobby, and back out onto Third Avenue. Suddenly, the actor who had been recognized by only a few at the start of the film now had to be ushered through the energized crowd, who were rushing to greet the "kid" they'd all just rooted for as if he were their own brother.

The crowd spilled out onto the sidewalk as I was guided by the filmmakers to a waiting car at the curb. I stopped and looked back at my "new friends," with whom I had just spent 126 minutes. What I saw was an image I will never forget. Everyone, and I mean everyone, was doing the crane stance out by the street. Kids and adults, teenagers and grandparents, all doing their imitation, their own version of Mr. Miyagi's winning crane kick.

I got into the back seat of the car and Kamen was wholeheartedly mocking me, jokingly acting like a fanatic pounding on the window as if I were the Beatles leaving Shea Stadium. Avildsen said earnestly of the film and my performance, "Congratulations! It's really a terrific story." And Weintraub, in his unmistakable Brooklyn accent, called out to me, "We're gonna be makin' a couple of these!"

My mind was racing as the car drove up Third Avenue. I was trying to make sense of everything I had just experienced. I laughed to myself at what Jerry had said. I mean, I knew what it meant, but at the same time, what did that really mean? "A couple of these." Two is a couple, three is a crowd, four is too many?

To be honest, as I sit here today, I don't think Jerry or anyone could have ever imagined that the legacy of *The Karate Kid* would still be going and growing for thirty-eight years, with no end in sight. The pop-culture relevance and staying power of the *Karate Kid* franchise never ceases to amaze me, and I am humbled at every chapter.

Let's take a quick look at "a couple of these," as Jerry Weintraub predicted. . . .

First, of course, there was the original. Then there was *The Karate Kid Part II*, released in 1986, followed by *The Karate Kid Part III* in 1989 (both starring yours truly). An animated series followed on NBC that same year. Then came *The Next Karate Kid* in 1994, which launched Hilary Swank's career. But we're not done yet. Let's jump about sixteen years to the 2010 *Karate Kid* remake with Jaden Smith and Jackie Chan, which was another box-office success at that time. I would say that constitutes "a couple of these." Wouldn't you?

But wait, there's more! A Broadway musical adaptation of the original film is currently scheduled to hit the Great White Way in 2023. With a book by the original screenwriter, Kamen, and music by Tony Award–level composers and producers, *The Karate Kid: The Musical* is on the way! Of course it is. Why not?

And *now* . . . just to pour a little bit more relevance on top of what has already been highlighted: Currently, I am reprising the iconic role of Daniel LaRusso, thirty-eight years later, in the critically acclaimed, Emmy-nominated, worldwide-hit television series *Cobra Kai,* which co-stars William Zabka, who portrayed LaRusso's nemesis, Johnny Lawrence, in the original *Karate Kid* film. It is a rivalry series that dives into the gray areas of both of these characters when their paths cross for the first time in decades.

The show originated on YouTube Premium in 2018 and was an instant hit, with fans and critics alike. The cherry on top is that the entire series was then licensed by Netflix, which relaunched the first two seasons to an even wider global audience in August 2020. It immediately became a smash hit. As I write this, I've just finished filming the fifth season of *Cobra Kai.* "A couple of these," huh? Boy, if I knew then what we know now, I still wouldn't have been prepared for this truly amazing voyage.

Lightning would strike in the summer of 1984, and it continues to strike and engage new fans around the world and across the generations. I knew I felt something magical that night at the Baronet in New York City. But I had no idea to what level. Daniel LaRusso was about to change my life. And that life . . . has been all the richer for it.

CHAPTER ONE

Becoming the Kid

It was late spring 1983. *The Outsiders,* my first major film, based on the classic S. E. Hinton novel, was finishing up a fairly successful run at movie theaters, and the notices for my performance as Johnny Cade were pretty solid. Still, to this day, it's one of my favorite roles on film. It was directed by Francis Ford Coppola and featured a cast that rivals any as far as launching big careers, including those of Cruise, Swayze, Lane, Lowe, and Dillon, to name a few. So, I was feeling pretty confident that things might be lining up in a good way for me as well. I was back home in New York on Long Island in the house where I grew up. My beloved New York Islanders were poised to win their fourth consecutive Stanley Cup championship, I was listening to Springsteen's *The River* album on a loop, and summer was right around the corner. I wondered what would be next.

It had been a few years since I was back in my old room full-time. A poster of Scorsese's *Raging Bull* still lived above my bed. A framed collage of Gene Kelly was a focal point too.

I wanted to be as cool and smooth as him when I was a little kid—an early influence from watching MGM movie musicals with my mom. I even took tap-dance lessons for a while in between Little League baseball games and working with my dad on Saturdays. My mom and I would often watch the four-thirty movie on WPIX, channel 11, after I got home from school. I was probably around six or seven years old when my love affair with movies and storytelling was born. My younger brother had taken more organically to the family laundromat and pump-truck businesses at that time. My mind was else-where, inside my imagination. In my early teens, between school plays and dance recitals, I would audition for commercials here and there. By the time I graduated high school I had landed two Bubble Yum spots and my first film role, in a movie titled *Up the Academy*. From there, I wanted to emulate my act-ing heroes. Brando, Pacino, De Niro, and a few New York Mets bobbleheads still peppered the bookshelves of my room. Springsteen and Billy Joel albums finished off the décor over yesteryear's shag carpet, which still covered the hardwood floor. This was where I had grown up. This was where I had daydreamed that I could "make it."

After *Up the Academy*, I lived in Los Angeles for two years coming off my one-season stint on ABC's *Eight Is Enough*. I was nineteen at that point. I stayed in California for the sec-ond year to further my craft, focusing on acting classes and auditions in between teen magazine shoots, before Coppola awarded me a role as one of the "greasers" in his newest film.

This was a *huge* break for me. A big win and step up in Hollywood street cred. And so, it was on that day that I made the decision to move back to New York after filming of *The Outsiders* was complete. I missed the East Coast energy and was eager to experience *The Outsiders'* release from home. Plus, New York City was only a train ride away, and this proved to be the right move for what was about to happen.

So there I was, sitting in my room on a faux-leather beanbag chair, probably with Martha Quinn in the background introducing a music video on my nineteen-inch Panasonic television, when the phone rang. I excitedly received the information about an upcoming audition for the starring role in a new Columbia Pictures movie. *Okay, that's cool.*

I found out they were making a film based on a newspaper article about a kid who was picked on and how martial arts helped him confront his bullies. *Sounds intriguing.*

It was being directed by the guy who made *Rocky. First the* Godfather *director and now the* Rocky *director. This is feeling really good now!*

The character's name was Danny Webber. *Hmmm, okay, I guess I could be a Webber.*

And the title of the script they were sending me was:

The-Karate-Kid

What? Seriously? Was this a cartoon? An after-school special? All I kept thinking was, *What a silly, lame-ass title. It must be a placeholder. Gotta be a working title, right? Okay, one thing at a time.* They were sending the script my way, and I would read it with an open mind over the weekend in preparation for my audition.

Here's what I remember about my first reading of Robert Mark Kamen's now classic screenplay. I recall connecting to the father-and-son elements and heart in the story right off the bat, even though I knew virtually nothing about Japanese culture. I didn't know what a bonsai tree was either, so that part was confusing. I found some of the high school story line characters a bit corny and stereotyped. As far as the fight scenes, it's always very difficult to grasp action sequences on the page, but I did feel they were unique and that the underdog dynamic was just so perfect in the hands of John G. Avildsen. *Rocky* was such an influential movie in my childhood. Perhaps the title was just a play on what they should have been calling it, *The Ka-Rocky Kid*. Actually, that is what Avildsen jokingly said the film could arguably be branded. Personally, I could not get past the fact that this major motion picture script would have such a ridiculous title. I mean, can you imagine? If I ever did get this part and the movie hit, I would have to carry this label for the rest of my life!!

Three days later, the sound of a train whistle blared as a westbounder entered the Babylon station. It was audition day, and there I was in my white Tom Petty concert shirt and my black Members Only–type jacket, stepping onto a Long Island Rail Road train to New York City. For some reason that I cannot explain today, that was my choice of wardrobe for this character. As the train made its way to Penn Station, I had the usual butterflies as I went over my audition scene. For reference, it was the scene that directly follows Mr. Miyagi's saving Daniel from the skeleton beatdown. The scene where Daniel discovers that Miyagi is a karate master. (The actual footage from that day lives on YouTube. Avildsen uploaded my first reading of the character years after the movie came out—it is intercut with Pat Morita's first-ever reading of Mr. Miyagi. It's really worth a look.)

Now, when you first go in to audition for a role, it's most often only with the casting director. What was unique about this scenario was that I was on my way to the director's home, an apartment on the Upper East Side of Manhattan, where I would meet with the Oscar-winning filmmaker John Avildsen one-on-one. As I rode uptown in my cab from Penn Station to Eighty-something Street, I wondered if, maybe, word of my performance in *The Outsiders* had gotten me past the first round. That had to be it, right? Not so fast. (Insert record scratch here.) When I arrived, I found a hallway packed with teenagers of all shapes and sizes. I reset my ego, took a deep breath, and made my way toward the apartment door at the end of the hall.

I distinctly remember hearing a few actors mocking the title as I navigated the crowded hallway, making fun of it as they snickered. It's interesting; in that moment I felt very validated on one level, but after spending the weekend with the script and preparing, I was now compelled to defend it. Sort of like sticking up for your brother. "Hey, I can make fun of him, but you can't." I was oddly offended by their negative comments about the title. How about that? Looking back, perhaps that was the first sign that I had a personal connection to this role, that it was somehow "destined" for me.

Finally, after a significant wait, during which I tried to remain loose and not give in to my pre-audition nerves, I heard my name called. It was my turn. I walked through John's apartment toward a back office, passing framed movie posters for *Save the Tiger*, *The Formula*, and *Rocky*. Something shiny and gold caught my eye on a shelf; I believe I was probably half looking for it. There it was. The Best Director Academy Award. An Oscar, live and in person. *Don't stare. Keep moving. Come on, you've worked with Coppola, just stay cool, Ralphie boy.*

I turned a corner to find John Avildsen, a man of small physical stature, reading glasses on the tip of his nose, sitting with a large JVC-type video camera pointed right at me as I entered. He was shooting my every move and our full conversation. He offered me a seat. I had the script in my lap, and he began to explain the plot of the movie from beginning to end, never taking the camera off me. He was capturing my every reaction. He then focused on the details that led to the audition scene. I tried not to be self-conscious that he was filming me and not the character at this point. Later I would recognize this as the way he documented my behavior. It was all part of the audition process. (Once again, the footage from this exact experience lives on YouTube.)

Then it was time to read the scene. I was feeling pretty good with the material, and the dialogue seemed to fit nicely in my mouth. In hindsight, probably another sign that this role was a good match. I just played it as naturally as I could, being honest with my reactions, allowing my East Coast cockiness to bleed through. We only read it once. That was it. No adjustments. No notes. He lowered his reading glasses and said in an impressed, almost surprised tone, "Wow, you're a good actor." Now, that's never a bad thing to hear on the first date. A proud feeling of jittery excitement was building in my chest. Then what really put it over the top for me was when he ended the audition meeting with "I can't guarantee anything for certain, but if I were you, I'd start taking some karate lessons." That got me up and out of the chair with a jolt. A pretty damn good sign, don't you think?

I left John's apartment with a spring in my step as I passed by the few remaining audition candidates and title-mockers. Out on Eighty-something Street, I hit the corner, and instead of getting a return taxi, I just decided to run down Fifth Avenue toward Penn Station. I didn't know what to do with myself. I had no cell phone to call anyone. It was 1983, people! I was too pumped with adrenaline to flag down a cab. Those fifty city blocks to Penn were an absolute blur. On the train ride back home to Long Island, I was beginning to fantasize about playing the part. Like Balboa running up the steps of the Philadelphia Museum of Art. Clearly, I was getting way ahead of myself, but hey, it's my imagination and I'll make it up if I want to!

They say "the waiting is the hardest part" (my second Tom Petty reference), and that proved to be true for me in the weeks and months ahead. The feedback my agents received from the casting office was excellent, and Avildsen even had me back twice to read with actresses for the role of Daniel's love interest, Ali Mills. (More on that later.) But still no offer. I thought for sure I'd nailed this on day one, judging by John's reaction in person. I had taken his advice and attended a jiujitsu martial arts class near where I lived on Long Island. I made sure my reps got this information to him, letting him know about my dedication and that I was following his lead. Soon after, he called me on the phone himself. Excited to hear directly from him, I braced myself for what I thought might be the official word. Nope! He wanted me to meet the screenwriter, Robert Mark Kamen. Robert had been trained in Okinawan Goju-Ryu karate (Miyagi's karate), and I guess he and John wanted to see what I could do. It had been some time since my first audition, so while I was on the phone, I felt the need to ask him the question that was hanging: "Am I going to get the part?" His answer was clear, noncommittal, and quintessentially Avildsen. "Listen, unless I run into a young Spencer Tracy between here and LA, you're the first choice right now." Okay, well, there is only *one* Spencer Tracy. Not that I would ever think that I was a better actor than Spencer Tracy, but what are the odds there'd be a "young" one? I took it as it was: undefined optimism.

I met Kamen at his apartment in New York City. He spent time with me going over some basic karate stances and circle movements, blocks, and strikes. This was the foundation for what would become wax on and wax off, etc. He sized me up right away. I later learned he described me as a skinny string bean of a kid, "obnoxious" but "sweet," and notably lacking in physical prowess. I guess that made me the perfect karate underdog. Within days we heard from the Columbia Pictures business affairs department. An offer was being made. But not the type of offer I was expecting.

The studio was offering a screen test deal, and it included two potential sequels. In other words, a three-picture deal. This was the beginning of that era of "tying up" actors in an early contract in the event a film became a franchise. However, a test deal means you do not have the part unless they pick up your option after a screen test. Bottom line being, more hoops and, more important, more time and chances for the young Spencer Tracy to eventually show up. I was flattered and frustrated all at the same time. I recall attempting to limit the test deal to only the one film at hand, but it was a "take it or leave it" scenario, and I had little leverage at that point in my career. So, for those fans who for years have asked, "Why *Karate Kid Part III*?"—you now have the answer. On the flip side, if it weren't for the "second sequel," there may never have been the hit *Cobra Kai* series. The creators of the show love having the canon from that third film to use in the show's plot lines. You see, with this storied franchise, even the shortcomings wind up giving back.

Once the test deal was finalized, I was soon on a plane to Los Angeles. They put me up at the Sheraton Universal. It was in close proximity to the Burbank Studios, which were occupied by both Warner Bros. Pictures and Columbia Pictures. It was home base for me for the next few weeks. Every morning, at the crack of dawn, there'd be an energetic knock on my door. I'd groggily open it up to find a hyper-enthusiastic '80's buff-ster with "Body By Jake" stretched across his T-shirt. He'd run me through a vigorous boot-camp program in my hotel room, which left me fairly limp and queasy as the morning sun bled through the crack in the aged curtains. Apparently, Avildsen and Kamen felt this "string bean of a kid" needed to ramp up for the task at hand and organized this eye-opening program. I negotiated myself out of having to continue the early-morning physical wake-up calls once my schedule expanded. Consequently, I never did achieve that Jake-like body. But Avildsen kept me busy in many other ways. He had set me up with a daily itinerary of martial arts training, co-star auditions, readings, BMX bike lessons, and soccer-ball-juggling lessons.

My days were full but there was no screen test in sight . . . so far. I was devoted to the work schedule but still technically unemployed. I would report to producer Jerry Weintraub's Bungalow One on the studio lot every morning to get my itinerary and would run into various department heads for the film. Cinematographer, production designer, location manager, you name them. Everyone treated me as if I had the part. Now, there was a lot of casting going on for the other roles, so I just assumed all the screen tests would happen together and then the cast would be locked, options would be picked up, and the role would officially be mine. But even so, it became increasingly difficult to not think everyone who passed me by looked like a young Spencer Tracy.

There was one distinct day when I ran into Charlie Sheen. I was on my way out of a casting session and he was hovering outside, off the corner of Bungalow One. *That's weird. What's Charlie doing here?* I knew him through his brother Emilio Estevez, whom I worked with on *The Outsiders*. We spoke a few friendly words of recognition as we passed each other. I wasn't really sure why he was there since I'd never witnessed him come in to read. Maybe they were waiting for me to leave first? I moved on with my day, though it did hang in the back of my mind. I learned as time went on that Charlie had indeed been a candidate for "my" role. As was Robert Downey Jr., whom I also knew from the past. Add a C. Thomas Howell to those two, and that was the trio that was considered, as I learned later. Oh, yeah, and I also got wind that Clint Eastwood was doing a push for his son Kyle. I'm sure there were many others, but those are the names that were officially in contention, with me remaining in first position. I was beginning to grow frustrated waiting for this "unofficial" journey to play itself out.

The casting fog eventually cleared up very quickly when the perfect ingredient was added to the mix. It all accelerated once I was connected with Pat Morita. The magic made in heaven. I will elaborate on this in much further detail in the next chapter. But for now, I'll just say that it was clear that any casting hesitations completely disappeared once Pat and I got in the same room. This appeared to seal the deal, and screen tests were scheduled right away. They played out like a regular production shooting day on the Columbia soundstage with rehearsals, costumes, makeup, and hair. This was, essentially, a formal screen test for the studio executives so they could view the footage the next day and officially sign off on the leads in their movie. The day had come, and although I'd felt like I had the part for weeks now, this was for all the marbles! I normally would be very nervous before a final test like this one, but that wasn't the case on this day. I was quite calm, if not overconfident, since I was the only actor testing for the Daniel role. Not to mention Weintraub, Avildsen, and the production staff had been addressing me as Daniel since I arrived in LA. Pat Morita and Elisabeth Shue also tested with me on that day. I realized the dragging on was all a formality that hinged greatly on the studio executives' witnessing my chemistry with my co-stars, coupled with the usual studio system politics.

It was late September by that point, and fortunately, it didn't take long to get the final verdict. I think it was the next day when I got the call and, for the first time, heard the words that I still hear to this day: "*You're* the Karate Kid!" I still cringed at the sound of the title, though I would be lying if I said I wasn't thrilled with the happy news. I received the production script later that afternoon with a more formal rehearsal schedule and the cast names inserted. It was awesome validation. But the moment it really sank in, the point when I knew it was an absolute done deal, was when I noticed in the new script that the last name *Webber* had been replaced with *LaRusso*. The new, customized last name made it all the more real and personal. Adding a few vowels to a surname somehow made it my own. I mean, Webber could have been Spencer Tracy, right? But LaRusso solidified Macchio. I embraced that victory and shifted everything into high gear.

The first thing I needed to figure out was my housing. Where would I stay for the next three months that would feel less like a hotel room? Someone suggested the Chateau Marmont, but I frowned on that option since it was where John Belushi had died of an overdose. Too disturbing. Instead, I chose the Beverly Comstock, only to find out one week later that's where Freddie Prinze shot himself. Good to be back in Los Angeles!

The start date for filming was scheduled for the end of October and we were in full prep mode. I would spend hours a day with our martial arts choreographer/stunt coordinator, Pat E. Johnson. He would train Pat Morita and me together in Okinawan-style karate. The Cobra Kai clan would train separately in their more aggressive style. In later weeks, we would be put together as fight sequences were built. Everyone loved working with Pat Johnson, who would wind up playing the tournament referee in the film. One field trip we took during those rehearsal weeks was to an actual martial arts tournament. That's where I was first exposed to how a competition actually worked and witnessed the intensity of the contests. This is one of the coolest components of being an actor: having the opportunity to submerge yourself in another world. To step into the shoes and the mindset of a culture or environment that may be out of your comfort zone. Or at the least enter a scenario that is unfamiliar and then make it your own through the character's experience.

The tournament was exciting. You couldn't help but become engrossed in what was on display in front of you. But LaRusso is such an outsider in our story, Avildsen and I really didn't incorporate too much of the tournament knowledge I absorbed that day into Daniel's character development, the thought being that the more Daniel didn't fit in, the more of an underdog he would be. John was very keen on creating that dynamic in the film, and I followed his lead.

Back at the studio stages in our makeshift dojo, I'd hear, "AGAIN . . . AGAIN . . . AGAIN," after we'd run each fight sequence. Avildsen was a stickler for repetition. We'd do them over and over and over. His mantra was "The more you know it, the faster you do it, the better we see it." He'd shoot each sequence on video and edit it, then we'd rework it and change it, and we'd rework it one more time. It was exhausting and sometimes frustrating but very tough to argue with his process. He had *Rocky* as leverage. Plain and simple, it worked! And boy, did it pay off.

In between training and fight rehearsals, we would head out to the actual filming locations or the stages where sets were being built to do scene work—once again, with John shooting every waking moment on videotape. Even my bike training and soccer training would be documented. He wanted me to be skilled at soccer and do super-cool tricks with a bike. For the record: decent at soccer, sucked with the bike. At night, on my own time, I would comb through my script, familiarizing myself with scenes, when startling realizations would come to mind. Not the least of which was, *Oh, shit, I use a fork at Chinese restaurants!* I began religiously ordering Asian food in an attempt to better learn the fine art of handling chopsticks. Picking up a piece of California roll was one thing . . . but catching a fly? *That's* another story! (Which I'll share later.) Finally, I did get the lowdown on bonsai trees when I visited the prop department. They had a nursery area with tons of them waiting for their turn to be used in the movie. You've got your junipers, your ficuses, your elms. Each one different, with its own temperament. If I only knew how distinctively unique they were, I would have suggested opening little huts to sell them in every mall in America. Oh, wait, what? Damn!

The rehearsal period was winding down, with the first day of production looming. In the past, I would often feel I wasn't ready by the time we got to the first day of shooting. Like I needed more time. Or I didn't know what I was doing or who this character truly was. But this was different. I had the feeling that I'd already slipped deep into the skin of this guy and we kind of shared a brain despite any differences. Defining the person of Daniel LaRusso was a process born back in my New York City audition that grew throughout the pre-production rehearsals. Avildsen allowed that to happen by guiding me and fostering nuanced behavior within Kamen's well-crafted script. We all collaborated on creating this truthful and relatable underdog with an East Coast edge. As an actor you often want to "disappear" into a role. You feel you can demonstrate your range by losing yourself in the character, so eventually, you're almost one. In the case of Ralph and LaRusso, that happened, but it was more about enhancing the similarities and then defining the differences. In this circumstance, "disappearing" meant not being able to discern where Ralph ended and LaRusso began. I recognize this now, whereas I wasn't so aware of it back then. I believe that is what led to one of the most honest and natural performances I have ever given.

There is a sweet toughness to LaRusso. He has this bravado that came naturally to me, drawn from my own experiences of being one of the smallest in my class and certainly looking so young for my age. I built up a defense to any teasing I would experience in junior high and high school. I'd act "tough" and confident to plow through any insecurities. That's where LaRusso's cockiness came from for me. With vulnerability and innocence always beneath any tough exterior. He certainly has more of a temper than I do and is way more knee-jerk defiant than I am. For example, if I got my ass kicked by a motorcycle-riding, leather-jacketed karate gang the first time . . . I would more than likely leave well enough alone. Then again, that mindset doesn't make for an exciting movie concept. It's much more fun if the protagonist doesn't let it go and possesses that feistiness. That plays currently into the *Cobra Kai* show as well. It's interesting to see how as a grown man LaRusso has evolved. Those same character traits become amplified. He dives deeper emotionally when it comes to his family and his heartfelt respect for Miyagi's legacy. Yet his bold defiance grows more intense when wounds are reopened by his old nemesis.

Now, I referenced that scene with motorcycles and ass-kicking from *The Karate Kid* specifically for a reason. Because that was the scene scheduled as first up on day one of principal photography. We started our forty-two-day shooting schedule with a split day: one daylight scene and one nighttime scene. The location was the beach at Leo Carrillo State Park in Malibu, California. We started at twelve noon with soccer by the surf and flirting with Elisabeth Shue. Once the sun set, it was all motorcycles and ass-kicking by William Zabka. That exact date?

October 31, 1983.

Halloween! Is that irony or foreshadowing or what? Think

about it. How many movies *not* about Halloween have as many pop-culture threads about that specific day? It runs deep in the *Karate Kid* cosmos, with visions of polka-dot shower-curtain costumes and angry skeleton gangs. Who knew on that day what was on the launchpad for this little, modestly budgeted underdog movie? On a sunny Monday afternoon in Southern California, we began capturing our story on film for the world to see. I eagerly juggled a soccer ball as I made my way down to the shooting location. The first setup was an establishing shot of us "kids" playing soccer on the beach. And it was there where I heard Avildsen call out for the first time, with bullhorn in hand . . .

"*The Karate Kid*, day one. . . . Camera's set . . . aaand ACTION!"

CHAPTER TWO

Soulful Magic

In the beginning, no one, and I mean *no one*, wanted Pat Morita to portray Mr. Miyagi.

What now seems a crystal-clear choice was initially a contested one. The movie studio, the producers, and their casting departments were scouring the Asian actor database (or whatever constituted a database in 1983) for strong actors who could convincingly pull off portraying the karate sensei and mentor for young Daniel-san. The focus was on the dramatic side of the character. Finding an actor of range and depth who would be authentic. One who had the look and feel of a true martial arts master but could also reveal a warm and caring side. This would need to be an accomplished thespian of serious proportions. This was no job for a lightweight. And definitely not for a comic.

Certainly, there had to be someone who fit the bill, right? But every single road led to another dead end. Mr. Miyagi was nowhere to be found. What they were looking for was not out there. And to that point, almost everyone was guilty of jaded

closed-mindedness. Including myself. Guilty of drawing conclusions without facts or truth. Of having preconceived notions of who someone is based on our perception of what they
can do. As a kid growing up, I remember one of my teachers
often saying something like, "If you would just open your
eyes, sometimes the answer is right there in front of you."
Well, fortunately for all of us, John Avildsen and his casting
director, Caro Jones, fought the shortsighted system and kept
their eyes wide and their minds open. He was most definitely
out there. Right in front of us.

I grew up in the seventies watching mainstream television.
In junior high school, Tuesdays on ABC were *Happy Days* at
eight P.M., followed by *Laverne & Shirley*. *Mork & Mindy*
came along later. That was my home entertainment in between math, English, and Chips Ahoy! cookies. Or another
personal favorite, Entenmann's chocolate-covered donuts with
a tall glass of Dellwood Dairy milk (ice-ice-cold). So, when I
heard the news that Pat Morita had become a late-in-the-
game candidate for Mr. Miyagi, all I could think of was the
character Arnold from *Happy Days*. He was the Japanese cook
from Mel's Diner who would do shticky gags and deliver
sidekick-style jokes with a "Bah-hah-ha!" tag each and every
time. I said to myself, "This is going to be a disaster." I mean,
I loved Arnold; he'd had me smiling my whole childhood
when he was ribbing the Fonz on Tuesday nights. But as Mr.
Miyagi? Could he handle the depth of the character? Would

we buy him as the karate master? I half eye-rolled myself to sleep with this lame idea.

When I look back at my knee-jerk reactions to hearing the news of Pat as a Miyagi candidate, it's remarkably ironic. Actually, it's quite sobering, because at that time, I myself was in the on-deck circle of being victim to typecasting of my own, having to fight back the stereotypes and pigeonholing that come along with being too associated with one character or type of character. Today, at this current point in my life, having lived through these experiences over my career, I believe I would react differently from how I responded to hearing the news back then. I think I would have had a very specific understanding and therefore more open-mindedness. I look forward to diving deeper into my experiences in this area at a later point in this book.

At first, early in the Miyagi casting process, it seemed everyone wanted Toshiro Mifune. Mifune was a famous Japanese actor from many classic Akira Kurosawa films. When reading the *Karate Kid* script, if anyone mentioned Mifune for the role, it just seemed to make good sense. You could see it as a real, viable option. The issue was he spoke very little English, and in his audition (I got to see his tape), he played the role as an intense and dramatic sensei with Kurosawa sensibilities. Like he was in *Seven Samurai* or the like. Powerful, invested, passionate. But something was missing. An element that was necessary to fully round out the embraceable human side of the Miyagi character. This was why it didn't go any further despite so many initially championing Mifune for the role.

Caro Jones was John Avildsen's personal casting director. She cast both the Academy Award–winning *Save the Tiger* and *Rocky*. As the story goes, Caro brought in a tape of Pat Morita to John. Word got around about how much John loved Morita's take on the role. They were looking to share the tape with Jerry Weintraub. Jerry apparently knew of Pat from his early stand-up days in upstate New York. I can almost hear Jerry's voice in my head. "No way! There is no way that Borscht Belt comic is gonna be in this picture! I remember booking him as 'the Hip Nip' in the Catskills." (Side note: I learned from Pat that Lenny Bruce's mother gave him that title at the start of his stand-up career. I also learned that it was Redd Foxx who gave Pat his big break on *Sanford and Son* and a ticket out of the Catskills and onto big-time TV.)

Now, I wasn't there on this specific day, but I was told Jerry refused to see Pat for the role. John, a very persistent and often tireless personality, had other plans. He was in Jerry's office on another matter and just decided to throw the tape in the VCR and let it roll. Jerry was speaking and focused on something else when his eye caught the monitor's screen. A double take— it only took a few beats before his attention was drawn to what was playing on the tape. He turned to John, probably muttering some Jerry-esque phrase equivalent to "Holy shit!" and essentially loosened his grip and lifted the ban. It was that clear. The next step? Putting Daniel and Miyagi in a room together.

If you recall from the previous chapter, I "had the role" but didn't have the role at that point. These next few events happened pre–screen test. I remember John calling me in to meet with him and Pat Morita in his office and saying that I should bring my script, as we were going to read some scenes together. One of those scenes was the one I performed in my audition with John in New York City, so I was almost off book (fully memorized) on that one. I recall heading over to Bungalow One on the Columbia lot with my latest draft of the script tucked under my arm. Butterflies were lightly flying around my stomach, as would be the case at each and every milestone moment. I still had the aftertaste in my mouth of my initial reaction to hearing about Pat Morita. Nevertheless, I was trying to be optimistic. However, I could not ignore the disappointment I felt at not having an Oscar-caliber dramatic actor as the potential Miyagi. (More brilliant irony, as Pat would be nominated for Best Supporting Actor for his magnificent portrayal of Mr. Miyagi.) On the flip side of this, the Long Island kid in me was actually a little excited to meet Arnold from *Happy Days*! I mean, come on, this was pretty cool! So, when I entered the room, I put my best foot forward and tried with a clear mind to leave my preconceptions at the door.

I walked into John's office and Pat was already there, his back to me. John was setting up his video camera, and I believe they were speaking about Pat's family and his Japanese American heritage when I interrupted the conversation. John popped up and said something like "Hey, look who's here." He introduced Pat and me to each other. We smiled and shook hands, and I sat down on the couch adjacent to the chair Pat was sitting in. He was wearing a floral Hawaiian shirt. This was a staple in Pat's wardrobe for as long as I can remember. I don't recall our actual dialogue in those first moments, but that may be due to the fact that I was so struck by something that took me by surprise. Something unexpected. The first layer was being peeled away from what I thought I knew. His English was perfect. He was extremely polite and soft-spoken and very pointed with his thoughts and delivery. I was half-expecting to hear Arnold's obnoxious laugh, yet it was nowhere to be found. I was taken aback at his attention to detail when he spoke to John and me about Miyagi's character and backstory. As if the silly comic from TV would not have had those instincts or that ability. Then Avildsen instructed us to turn to the scene's page in the script. As we thumbed through, looking to locate the page, for some reason I thought this was the moment to let Pat know that I had watched every episode of *Happy Days*. It just hung out there in the air for a nanosecond (it felt like three minutes), then he nodded and smiled politely with his mind clearly on the task at hand. *Come on, Ralph! Timing, man. Focus on the audition.* Once the foolish embarrassment had vacated my head, I was prepared to launch into the scene. Thankfully, I had this one mostly memorized.

If you've ever wondered where the iconic Daniel LaRusso headband came from . . . it was born in the following moment.

At the top of the audition scene, the script called for Mr. Miyagi to dip a rag into a solution and apply it to the bruises Daniel received from the skeleton fight. Pat pulled out a "handkerchief" from his pocket and asked if he could use it as a prop. This handkerchief became the now famous *Karate Kid* headband. He carefully unfolded the cloth to show us the blue-and-white "rising sun" design and explained it was called a *hachimaki*, which translates to "helmet scarf." He explained to both John and me its significance in Japanese culture—how it represents perseverance, courage, and effort—and why he thought Miyagi would have this. John was on board, and we moved forward with the scene and the use of the *hachimaki* as a prop. Later on, during rehearsals, we discovered another moment. When Daniel offered to give it back, Miyagi told him, "You keep." This is a significant sign of respect, when an elder offers his own *hachimaki* to a student. We all collectively loved this idea and then came up with the plan that Daniel would only wear it when he trained in karate with Mr. Miyagi, and, of course, in the All Valley tournament. And that is how it came to be. Therein lies the truth of how the *hachimaki* made it onto my head and into the cinema history books.

Circling back to the scene reading with Pat, John positioned the camera and quietly called action. In the blink of an eye, I witnessed an instant transformation. I heard for the first time the one and only Miyagi voice. The cadence of his speech, the resonance—it was all there. The perfect-English-speaking guy vanished. The character of Arnold was not anywhere to be found or even in the furthest reaches of my imagination. Pat had it all. The beats, the rhythm, the tone. A transformation that buried all preconceived notions. He inhabited this role— he *was* Mr. Miyagi. The fact that I was off book allowed me to fully lock in and experience it. I snapped into the scene as Daniel LaRusso, and I can only describe it as . . . easy. Effortless from the first time we began the give-and-take.

"What kind of belt do you have?"
"You like? JCPenney, three ninety-eight."

The comic in him knew just how and when to add the spice of humor beneath the dramatic narrative. It was instinctual. And the importance of this Japanese American character was personal to him and was infused with such honesty and soulfulness. I was witnessing a moment of destiny. An actor who was born to play this role. And I was part of it. Something unique and rare both in life and on film. The perfect match.

There were still a bunch of hoops to jump through before we got to the formal screen test. We worked on other scenes, and John had the screenwriter, Robert Kamen, sit in on sessions to enhance any elements of the script. Robert was extremely well versed in Okinawan Goju-Ryu karate, and he would share his knowledge with Pat, which only enriched Pat's character development during this process. I would absorb as much as I could. I think this added to the ease with which we connected and slipped into the skins of these characters, and the natural chemistry that was so evident to everyone as we explored the nuances of scenes. I just felt it was easy to act with Pat. I couldn't really tell at that point, from the inside of it, how truly special it was. I only knew that it was easy. Even though I would later hear it described as magical.

Now, neither Pat Morita nor myself would ever be considered a model of elite athleticism. Not by any stretch of the imagination. (Yep, dad joke.) So, when it came to our first training session together, it was less than stellar. Not quite sure either of us could touch our toes without bending our legs in the beginning. But it was a process, and we were game to make the best of our limitations in flexibility. Our stunt fight choreographer, Pat Johnson, would train us in the classic fundamentals of Goju-Ryu. We even began the early choreography of the payoff scene that would take place in Mr. Miyagi's backyard: "Show me, wax on, wax off." John would come by and videotape the sessions to see how it was going. I was starting to feel pretty good about my progress, when John laid down a reality check, that it had to be a lot better and much faster to be convincing. Damn that *Rocky* movie! In truth, Pat and I worked our butts off on that specific sequence because we all knew the payoff of the chores' becoming self-defense moves was paramount in the story. It worked like gangbusters, and LaRusso's realization linking the unorthodox techniques later produced the first applause heard in the theater from audiences around the world. But it wasn't easy getting there, and we made many mistakes during training. Some of my fondest memories were the laughs Pat and I would have at our own expense. We would get the giggles like two kids in history class as the teacher was attempting to offer an important lesson. Fortunately for us, Pat Johnson, although a fierce competitor and accomplished martial artist, was a teddy bear at heart and made the Miyagi/Daniel training sessions some of my favorite time spent behind the scenes.

We had reached the day of our screen test, and Pat and I already felt at one with these characters and our already strong, familiar partnership. He was in costume, with his "Miyagi khakis," and I was appropriately "Jersey LaRusso" in my threads. Hair and makeup were done, and we hit our marks. We smoothly performed our well-rehearsed scenes on the Columbia soundstage, and they were captured on film for the official decision makers to see the next day.

And then, it was done. It was official. I always loved hearing Pat tell the story of how no one wanted to see him for the part and the way the phone call from Weintraub came in on judgment day. He'd parody Jerry's thick, brash Brooklyn accent, saying something like, "Hey, Pat! I almost made da biggest mistake ah my life. Congratulations, ya got da part of Meeyahgee." Ah, and what a sweet victory it was . . . for all of us.

Very often I will get asked what my favorite scene or line is from the movie. Choosing a favorite scene is difficult, as I really have a few that I love. But choosing the line? Well, that one's easy. I don't have to think twice about it. It is not the flashiest. It's not the coolest. And it certainly is not the most unique. However, it is all and everything of what is at the heart of the *Karate Kid* film. It's the moment when LaRusso is at a loss for words because of the generosity of his mentor. He sits in the driver's seat of the just-gifted yellow 1947 Ford convertible that Miyagi gave Daniel on his sixteenth birthday, replaying in his mind everything this surrogate father has done for him to that point. He turns and simply says, "You're the best friend I ever had."

It is one of the purest and most genuine line readings I can ever remember giving as an actor. And even to this day, I look at that as the benchmark for myself in honesty of performance. It was beautifully written and placed precisely at the right time in the story. The only thing richer than that was Mr. Morita's pitch-perfect response, "Ah . . . you . . . pretty okay too." The emotional weight and breadth of those moments is what keeps this film from being narrowly categorized as an "eighties movie." They stand the test of time, and I credit a bit of that to the soulful magic that Pat and I shared.

There were other examples involving my working with Pat that affected me deeply. Being informed about another culture and educated on a dark time in American history was one of the richest experiences I had in making this film. And nothing was more moving and impactful than what I discovered during the "Miyagi drunk scene." Prior to rehearsing this part of the film, I didn't know anything about the Japanese internment camps, and that Pat himself, as a boy, spent a few years in two such camps, something he revealed to me during the preparation and actual filming of this scene.

The Karate Kid was the first mainstream Hollywood movie to address these events. I am proud of that. It was and is a subject that deserves more attention, and I myself didn't grasp it during my time in high school; I don't remember whether it was even taught in the curriculum. For those who are not aware, following the attack on Pearl Harbor, it was the policy of the US government that people of Japanese descent be interned in isolated camps. They were labeled "relocation centers." It was particularly praiseworthy that Robert Kamen had added this to Miyagi's backstory, shining a light on this stain on our country's history while adding depth and a greater degree of understanding of the void in Mr. Miyagi's life. He had lost his wife and unborn child due to complications at birth during their internment.

For many reasons, the relevance of this scene was on another level for Pat, and I felt privileged to participate in that part of our story. It was, as he would often call it, his "Oscar scene."

There is a moment at the end of this particular scene that is noteworthy, and one of my favorite moments and transitions in the film. It was discovered on the day of filming as we were blocking the scene to set the camera's placement. And all the credit in the world goes to John Avildsen. At the end of the scene, after Daniel puts Mr. Miyagi to bed and learns of the tragedy and heartache in his mentor's past, the script simply stated, "Daniel exits." Upon seeing this in the blocking rehearsal, after all of the emotional meat of the scene had been shot earlier that night, John suggested to me (actually, he told me) that I should stop, turn, and bow to Miyagi before I left. I fell in love with this direction the moment I heard it. It played so beautifully when we shot it, and it's even more emotionally charged on the screen. It is a vibrant example of how filmmaking is one of the most collaborative art forms on the planet. With Bill Conti's brilliantly orchestrated "Training Hard" composition underscoring the transition, Daniel heads out to train himself with heartfelt motivation that thrusts us toward the climax of the movie. As a fan, to this day, I still get all the feels every single time I watch it.

The ridiculous irony here is that the studio wanted the whole Miyagi backstory scene cut. They felt it took too long. Even the editor suggested it be eliminated, that it stopped the momentum of the plot and slowed the pacing at a point when it should accelerate to a climax. What a head-scratcher that was. The studio's main concern was that with the movie running over two hours, they would lose a daily screening time and, essentially, money in the process. The shorter the movie, the more times you can screen it. Kamen and Avildsen fought back, explaining how it would rip away the heart of the entire piece if the scene was taken out. The studio still complained about the 126-minute running time. But as Avildsen explained it to me, "They all shut up once we screened it for them with an audience." Thankfully, the artists' vision stayed true and the power of the people prevailed! Not to mention, Pat did get that well-deserved Oscar nomination.

What was truly extraordinary about Pat's process was his ability to turn it on and off like a switch. He could snap in and out of character without missing a beat or losing any quality or credibility. He would be deep into an emotional moment, and when the camera cut, at any time, he would launch into a barrage of fart sounds or deliver a cross-eyed one-liner with a zing. All for a good laugh to break any tension in the room. Or perhaps on a deeper level, because of the often-described comic's need for attention. But I think he got the greatest reward out of cracking me up to the point where I would lose my concentration. I did not have his gift for snapping in and out seamlessly. And the truth is, very often, keeping me off-balance yielded some of my truest interactions, since I wasn't "in my head" and editing my own choices. I would be more present, which was a good lesson to learn as a young actor and one I am still refining to this day. Yes, Pat really was a comic at heart . . . and with a ton of heart.

He would always affectionately call me "Ralphie." Probably the only one besides my mom who took ownership of that. "Hey, Ralphie, Ralphie, come on, let's go grab some sushi," he would say. I would go for the cooked stuff and he would go for the raw stuff. The more we went, slowly but surely, I would grab some raw stuff and he would appease me and throw back some of the cooked stuff. There was that give-and-take. A yin and yang, even when ordering food. There was a respect that we instinctively and mutually had for each other. The specialty in our relationship was through our characters' bond and that magic we shared as performers. A genuine connection of the heart that we both felt and cherished.

After making the films, we would fall out of touch a bit. Life gets in the way. But Pat would always be the first one to pick up the phone and check in. I'd get these great messages on my Message-Minder 1800 answering machine. *Hey, Ralphie, what's up? It's Unca Popzi! Whatcha been up to? Miss you. Call me. I love your ass, baby!* And he'd tag it with his signature laugh every time. I can hear it now as if it were yesterday. Man, I wish I'd kept those tapes.

As years went by—decades, for that matter—*The Karate Kid* grew bigger in the pop-culture pantheon, and so did the legacy of Mr. Miyagi. It was only after Pat had passed that I was truly able to see the scope of that character's effect on the world. My screen partner was no longer here, but luckily for us Mr. Miyagi will always remain. Pat passed away in November 2005 on Thanksgiving Day. Odd and extraordinary, considering how thankful I am to have had him in my life. I remember Kamen calling me after hearing about Pat's passing and saying something like, "This feels like Abbott has lost his Costello. You and Pat are one of the most revered screen partnerships in

American cinema." And I will always have that, and we will always share that. You and I, the audience, the fans. We keep that legacy alive.

As I got older, I was able to clearly recognize how rare a cinematic partnership like the one Pat and I shared was. The impression that we made together as Mr. Miyagi and Daniel-san never dissipated. This is why it was important to me to be sure the connection between Daniel and Miyagi continued with the *Cobra Kai* series. Fortunately, the creators of *Cobra Kai* (Jon Hurwitz, Hayden Schlossberg, and Josh Heald) saw it the same way. There was no resistance when I told them of my need to have the Mr. Miyagi character woven into the series throughout its run. In fact, it was always their intention to honor Mr. Miyagi in the series.

The more we talked, I would speak further of how imperative it was to me that Miyagi's essence be felt in adult Daniel LaRusso's life. How we should feel his presence in the story and it should even inform elements in the storytelling. What would that void be like for Daniel (and his family) as they navigated the world without his mentor and friend? Well, like I said, it was always their intention, and they have executed it brilliantly. Combining the use of flashbacks from the original films and Miyagi stories told by characters in the series, those components have been infused into every season of the show. They are some of my favorite sequences and moments. Jon, Josh, and Hayden have labeled it all "the Miyagiverse." Essentially, any character or story point that took place during Mr. Miyagi's life in the original film and its sequels can be canon for *Cobra Kai*.

This is particularly effective in season 1 when adult Daniel visits Mr. Miyagi's grave site seeking the balance that has been absent in his midlife, inspired to go back to his karate roots and center himself. Or in season 3 when Daniel is at a point of self-doubt and journeys to Okinawa, Japan, looking for answers in the home country of his master. This was a direct callback to *The Karate Kid Part II*, where the history of Miyagi-Do and Mr. Miyagi's backstory were highlighted. The authenticity of this story and these characters was so important to Pat when making the sequel. As I alluded to earlier, he felt a great responsibility in representing his culture honestly and genuinely. Having the opportunity to dive back into this area during *Cobra Kai* was a favorite experience of mine.

I stopped by the *Cobra Kai* writers' room just as the staff was gearing up to map out the story for season 3. These folks are some of the most collaborative, receptive, and talented writers I have ever had the pleasure of working with. As we start each season, I like to offer my thoughts on one or two elements I am looking for in regard to Daniel LaRusso's character arc going forward. I was aiming to impart ideas that would support further color shadings and depth for my journey in the series. My main note for season 3 went something like this: "Teach me something that we don't know about

LaRusso and have both the character and the audience learn unexpected details that add complexity to his life." This was something I felt had been so beautifully done with the Johnny Lawrence character but not as much with the LaRusso character, at least up to that point. They were already way ahead of this, and their answer was in Daniel's two-episode excursion to Japan—specifically, Okinawa. Side note: We filmed *The Karate Kid Part II* in Hawaii, so this was the first time I actually got to set foot in the land of Miyagi. To say this was a series highlight for me would be an understatement.

Tamlyn Tomita and Yuji Okumoto reprised their roles in those two poignant episodes respectively as Daniel-san's love interest Kumiko and nemesis Chozen. Both of these characters live deep within the Miyagiverse, so this was a perfectly crafted area to explore and expand on. Pat had a great affinity for both of these actors, so it was particularly rewarding to be creating this opportunity in the series. The arc of the Chozen character enlightens LaRusso and provides a better understanding of Miyagi-Do karate. It dives into the origins and some of the secrets that Mr. Miyagi never shared and why he withheld them. I recall a moment when we were rehearsing and Yuji said something to the effect of "Man, Pat would have loved all of this." We shared a deep understanding, and I held his gaze with a knowing nod as we both reflected. I felt a lump in my throat and a rush of emotion just knowing what it would mean to Pat that his friends were carrying on the traditions. I only wished in the moment he could have experienced this in person. Yuji's performance was wonderful. He absolutely knocked it out of the park, and his Miyagi-Do arc propelled LaRusso's story line both later that season and beyond. There was always a palpable feeling that Pat's spirit was there, and Mr. Miyagi's legacy informs us every time we shoot this type of scene in *Cobra Kai*.

Here's another meaningful example. Kumiko reads letters to Daniel left behind by Mr. Miyagi, which open his eyes to some unknown truths about Mr. Miyagi and the inspiring effect Daniel had on his life. All of this at a point when Daniel feels inferior and lost. Miyagi's words, through Kumiko, provide Daniel the inspiration to navigate the hurdles in front of him. In essence, he's being guided from beyond by his father figure. This scene was wonderfully written, and it was beautifully played by Tamlyn, who was very close to Pat. He meant a great deal to her and her own Okinawan heritage. She and I shared a unique emotional connection during the filming as actors, friends, and characters. It was twofold, both artistic and personal. When we finished the letter-reading scene and the crew was wrapping up all of the cameras and equipment, we embraced in the middle of the Japanese courtyard we were in and just held each other there tightly for a significant moment as if we were not alone. It was just the three of us. His presence was felt the whole evening by our characters and by us. Once again, Pat Morita and Mr. Miyagi had graced the *Karate Kid* universe.

I believe Pat is watching this current resurgence and

witnessing the soulful magic living on in his Miyagiverse. I can only imagine hearing the answering machine message he'd leave now—*Hey, Ralphie, it's Unca Popzi. I'm always right here when you need me. Congrats, Daniel-san! You know I love your ass, baby!*

Arigato, my friend.

You are forever my sensei. . . .

CHAPTER THREE

Strawberry Shortcake and the Cannoli

Opposites attract—a cliché or a proven statement? Who belongs together? What defines "a cute couple"? Does social class have a hand in it? Does geography play a part? More important in this circumstance—what looks great on camera? In this specific case, the answers to these questions lie in a pastry box.

Sometime between my first meeting with Avildsen in New York City and my visit with Kamen in his apartment, I was called in to read with a top candidate for Ali, the female lead of the movie. I was excited to be asked to participate in a chemistry read like this, as it was another solid indication that I might actually get the part. Like I was on the other side of the judgment line, officially the director's first choice. Or at least it felt that way. When you are called in to audition other actors for other roles, in most cases, it provides you a sense of confidence. But in this case, since I was specifically playacting with the female love interest in the movie, my leading-man insecurities were bubbling up under the surface, neutralizing any overconfidence. There was not a wealth of experience to draw from here in regard to on-screen courtships in past films or television series. In *The Outsiders*, Johnny Cade never had a girlfriend, and the one or two platonic dates my *Eight Is Enough* character participated in were superficial at best. This was new territory for me and my neophyte screen romance skills. This story had a teen-love relationship that actually gave birth to the plot's main conflict in the movie. And amazingly, it has still informed the conflict decades later in the *Cobra Kai* series. So, this was an even more significant casting decision than I knew at that time.

Heading up to John's apartment, I wrapped myself in my Long Island/New Jersey–tough armor and put on my best ladies' man swagger. I believe Elisabeth Shue was already there when I arrived. Was I late? That's highly unlikely, as I always pride myself on my punctuality. To this day, I am rarely, if ever, late. Perhaps Avildsen wanted to work with her on the scenes beforehand and scheduled me to join in later. Yep, I'll go with that. That's the best of my memory and I'm sticking to it. Now, what I'm not foggy about is my first encounter with Lisa. Yes, I know you're thinking, *Wait, it's Elisabeth, right?* Yes, this is true, but I was never introduced to an Elisabeth. I only knew Elisabeth as Lisa. John called her Lisa, I called her Lisa, and I am pretty sure she called herself Lisa. We were all on a nickname basis from the start. Kind of the same with William Zabka, whom I have only called Billy since 1983. (Stay tuned, next chapter.)

As I attempted to be in control of my coolness, I clearly re-call noticing Lisa's distinctive laugh, which she often would sprinkle in between her responses (still the same today). Not to mention her cuteness and the denim jacket she wore to the audi-tion. I don't know why, but I especially remember the jean jacket. Maybe it was because it was almost identical to the one Johnny Cade wore in *The Outsiders*. Conceivably, I made that connection at the time and that's why it always stuck. (You can see part of my first scene reading with Lisa on YouTube, as Avildsen posted that as well in 2011.) John was, typically, vid-eotaping our every interaction from the moment I walked in, framing his two-shot of our first introduction and the nervous chatter that ensued before we settled into the reading and acting out of the scenes. (The YouTube clips are only edits of the actual scenes as we performed them.) He shot different angles of each take, which he would then edit together later. The more we read the scenes, the more comfortable I became, and the more honest our interactions were. I still felt a bit insecure, but my confi-dence was building, which led to my sense of freedom to ad lib. This was something that John would encourage, and there was playacting and improvising during and in between the written scenes. Some of it worked and some of it did not, but this defi-nitely took some pressure off the audition process for me, and it became playful. I believe that was John's intention all along.

This seemed to work well, as I became much less self-conscious and settled into a more relaxed groove. In one par-ticular pass of a scene, when I asked for her name, Lisa responded with the now famous/infamous "Ali . . . with an I." That was on the page in the script. She then in turn asked me the same question and I replied with my written line, "Daniel." In that moment I decided to tag it ". . . with an L." She laughed, I laughed. This giggling went on for a beat, then she would turn to exit the scene. As I eyed her walking away, something pushed me to button it with a quite self-assured sotto voce delivery of "Def-in-ite-ly." I don't think those organic additions would have happened had I not felt the self-confidence to deliver them in the moment. Mission accomplished, Mr. Avildsen. Well done. A few weeks later, in a revised draft of the script, both "Daniel . . . with an L" and "Definitely" had been incorporated.

I'm a little bit vague on how this next event happened and whether this was the same day or if Avildsen had us back a second time, but I recall having lunch with Lisa (a sandwich or something), sitting on the steps of one of the museums close to John's apartment on the Upper East Side. We were probably both early for a callback appointment and waiting for John to invite us in. We spoke a bit about our personal backstories, our families, and where we came from. Me, fairly working-class Long Island. She, slightly upper-class New Jersey, referring to the prestigious Columbia High School in New Jersey and a Massachusetts college or two. (She wound up going to both Wellesley *and* Harvard.) I kept my C+ average and basic high school diploma under wraps. And then there was discussion of soccer. I remember hearing about her and her brothers all being awesome at soccer. I sensed in her a very competitive tomboy nature underneath her unmistakable attractiveness. *Soccer? Really? Damn! LaRusso is good at soccer too.* If we indeed were awarded these roles, I'd be feeling the pressure—I would have my work cut out for me on the field as well as the karate mat. The underdog element of the character was firmly in my wheelhouse. The being accomplished in karate and soccer, not as much. But as you can see, one helped the other, and that may be one of the reasons Daniel LaRusso worked so well as a character we all rooted for.

Back in John's apartment, I remember Lea Thompson also came in to read. She and Lisa knew each other and were friends. At least it seemed that way. They embraced and laughed when they saw each other. They caught up for a minute as I awkwardly played witness to their friendship and familiarity. Lea was lovely and the scenes went well when we read them together. But Lisa was the match for Ali, and that was evident in Avildsen's reaction even as I read with both. Don't cry for my friend Lea; she has an impressive and thriving acting and directing career. And it's just spectacular irony that both she and Lisa are part of the universe of *Back to the Future,* the other blessed franchise that was born in that eighties-movie era.

I hung back in John's apartment after we had finished the session and was gathering my stuff when John looked at me and began to chuckle. He then smiled big and asked me what I thought of Lisa. I recall saying reading with her was really fun and noted, "I liked the improv stuff we did. She seems cool." He smiled wider and laughed a bit louder. He started shaking his head. I didn't know what that meant in that moment. Did I say the wrong thing? Did I suck? What? Then he tapped me on the cheek with his hand, still shaking his head, as if he had to break some kind of news to me. He then proceeded to say, "You have no business being with this girl"—his laughter grew some more—"but you two are perfect together and look terrific—like a strawberry shortcake and a cannoli."

When you think of it—this pastry analogy, I mean—it is acutely accurate. LaRusso and Mills. Macchio and Shue. One ethnically Italian: crispy and hard-shelled on the outside with a concentrated, dense sweetness on the inside. And the other so visibly all-American, with the airy softness of sophistication, natural and organic as the fruit and whipped-cream combination it represents. Both delectable. Both probably displayed on opposite ends of the bakery case. As if they need to cross the tracks to the other side of town in order to meet. I have always loved that description that John gave us. A clear visual definition of our couple-ness that also begs for a double espresso macchiato (my hot beverage of choice these days). Suffice it to say, Elisabeth Shue sailed smoothly through the screen test process and was officially *The Karate Kid*'s Ali with an I—her first major movie role in what has been a long and impressive career in film and television.

Daniel and Ali are a beloved teen couple galvanized in eighties cinema. When I look back at that time in American movie history, there was something distinct about how these young romances were presented. Whether it be in the John Hughes movies or *Back to the Future, The Karate Kid,* or others from that era, they were specific to that time. There was an innocence, an adolescent openness and vulnerability, that we don't often see as much in films today. Perhaps it was a simpler time. Perhaps it was a superficial representation, but it certainly had its place. I will explore this further in a future chapter, but I want to point out an element of my character in this film that was and is unique to LaRusso and Ali Mills.

It happened as we were shooting and in production. Specifically, when Lisa and I were improvising during a scene that took place in the high school cafeteria. It began with a suggestion from Avildsen. It addressed the vulnerability and insecurity of Daniel LaRusso and that East Coast toughness that I incorporated to mask any exposure of those character traits, some of which mirrored my own. We decided to put a "little voice" in Daniel's head where he would talk out loud when it concerned Ali. Sometimes this would be in her presence and other times it would play out when he was by himself or left alone to reminisce about her. This simple device was used exclusively in that relationship. These moments revealed self-doubt and reflective thoughts while endearing his inner voice to the audience and therefore making him all the more relatable.

In the cafeteria scene, it works as a front, a cover, when he learns that Johnny Lawrence is Ali's ex-boyfriend. It has this cocky air to it when Daniel learns of that information and quickly looks to the sky, answering his inner thoughts with "What? Wha . . . ? Oh yeah, you're right, you're right, I know." He then goes on to explain that it's his little voice letting him know he's crazy for talking to her, being that she dated the guy who just recently beat the crap out of him. When she proceeds to say that she and Johnny have been over for *weeks*, Avildsen tossed out a line pitch to me that inspired this tag of Daniel's: "Weeks? One week, five weeks, how many weeks is weeks?" In that second moment of self-talking, the cockiness takes a back seat and gives way to vulnerability and innocence. These shadings in character I believe became part of LaRusso's appeal and were something that felt fresh and in line with the movies of that time period.

My favorite example of this is in the restaurant scene with Daniel's mom, Lucille, portrayed so honestly by the wonderful Randee Heller. After Lucille leaves the scene, Daniel goes on talking to himself about Ali and her amazingness. We feel his confidence building on how she is "hot, definitely hot," and that she "buries Judy in a second" (his old flame from back in Newark, New Jersey). All the while the Cobra Kai gang is watching him from outside the restaurant's window, contemplating their revenge. I remember Weintraub and Avildsen both approaching me the next day to offer their praise after seeing the rushes (the morning footage of the scenes shot the day prior). They called it my best scene so far. They elaborated that the ad-libbed inner-voice reflections had my character's underdog likability jumping off the screen. There was still a long way to go, as this was early in production, but their compliments stuck with me and provided a nice gust of wind in my sails in the early days of filming.

I don't have an answer as to why the little voice and self-talking character traits never resurfaced in the sequels. I really wish they had. But there's always room to reestablish it in *Cobra Kai,* and we love to reveal those Easter eggs and callbacks that are woven into the show. One particular deleted *Karate Kid* scene that involved Lisa and me makes an appearance in season 4 of *Cobra Kai.* It is the omitted blueberry pie scene that immediately followed the cafeteria scene in the script. We filmed the scene, but it never made the cut. In the scene, Daniel is about to take his seat next to Ali, when Johnny Lawrence slips a piece of pie under him as he sits. Splat! With blueberry stuck to the ass of his pants, LaRusso peels off the paper plate covered in purple goop; walks over to Johnny, who is laughing with his cronies; and defiantly presses it onto Johnny's chest. A cafeteria riot breaks out and Ali once again bears witness to these boys battling over and around her. I think the scene was cut because of redundancy, but it's so awesome to have access to all the footage shot during the making of the original film. It will be selective memory that informs how adult Daniel and adult Johnny remember that specific incident. Their opposing viewpoints and perspectives will service how it's incorporated into *Cobra Kai.* I can't express how much fun it is to play the yesterday in the today of these characters. I had absolutely no idea back then. Not in my wildest imagination did I feel that these characters would be revisited more than three decades later.

No example of this rings truer than the case of Elisabeth Shue, whose character was unceremoniously written off in one line of dialogue at the beginning of *The Karate Kid Part II*. Yet Ali is still the stimulus behind the initial rivalry in *Cobra Kai*, and Lisa makes a highly anticipated and celebrated appearance in the finale of season 3. I will circle back to all of that soon, but I first want to showcase other highlights and a few shortcomings as a leading man in my rookie year of 1983.

At that time in my personal life, I was absorbed in a relationship with my girlfriend Phyllis. We had dated in puppy-love form a few years back before she went off to college. But around the time I was starting the movie, the relationship had stepped up a notch and true love was in the air. I was a novice in my adult dating experience, but I guess you can say I had very good instincts. Or maybe I was just lucky. Phyllis and I recently celebrated our thirty-fifth wedding anniversary. Okay, it was definitely both. The reason I set this up is to clarify where my heart was at when I wasn't prepping for or working on the film.

Actors are often asked about their behind-the-scenes relationships with their co-stars. One just assumes, "Of course they did." And yes, I have gotten that question more than a handful of times over the years in regard to myself and Lisa. Well, for those of you waiting for me to expound on any juicy details . . . Sorry, I got nothin' for ya. How boring, right? Okay, wait . . . let me think, just a minute. Yes, I remember now. Lisa and I did have one non-date during the rehearsal period before filming started. We went to see a movie together in Westwood. This was the town neighboring UCLA. It had a bunch of movie theaters and restaurants, so perhaps we grabbed dinner as well. Back then it was always a hot spot and the place to be on a movie's opening weekend.

The film we saw was called *All the Right Moves*. Its backdrop was football, so there were similarities since we were about to make a "sports movie" too. The film starred Tom Cruise and Lea Thompson as the story's young couple. As I noted earlier, Lea and Lisa were friends, and I knew Cruise, as we'd co-starred in *The Outsiders* together. So, there seemed to be a few good reasons why we'd take in this particular flick as we were in the getting-to-know-you phase of pre-production and "finding our characters." I don't remember the specifics of our conversations that evening, but the night out together only enhanced our on-screen chemistry and appeal. I had a great time.

However, I do recall being a little tentative and awkward when I was outside of the LaRusso character. I lacked the adult experience of being a gentleman to a lady. My devotion was elsewhere, but I couldn't help but be aware of Lisa's attractiveness and charisma. I mean, come on, it was Elisabeth Shue even before she was "Elisabeth Shue." The absence of my seasoned leading-man behavior kind of bled over into certain scenes in the romance department. I have always felt that this might be a minor shortcoming in my performance. Probably more in my head than anything else. You know, not being more experienced in those types of scenes. That being said, as I have mentioned in the past, the amateur-like, tough-guy innocence played a large part in framing LaRusso as a likable underdog. Phew! Man, am I glad *that* worked for me!

Back on Long Island, New York, the place that had all the rides and games was called Adventureland, on Route 110 in East Farmingdale. In *The Karate Kid* it was Golf N' Stuff in Norwalk, California, where the ultimate eighties teen-love amusement park movie montage took place. Golf N' Stuff is still there and boasts a place in movie history as Daniel and Ali's date-night spot. When we filmed the scenes, Lisa and I spent the day on bumper cars and trampolines, playing mini golf, going on water rides, and playing table hockey. This all culminated in those adorable photo booth pictures. Yeah, Avildsen was right. We did look terrific together. We were creating an endearing, iconic movie couple who would be embraced around the world. I just didn't know it yet. I remember we had a great time shooting that sequence and that Lisa just hated to lose any of the arcade games. And I mean not a little bit. She was tough. That competitive gene I wrote about was up front and center at Golf N' Stuff. I'm just glad I never had to face her in the All Valley tournament, let alone in one-on-one soccer.

The next night of shooting was the "get back the girl"

scene. This is when LaRusso realizes he jumped to conclusions without all the information regarding Johnny kissing Ali at the Encino Oaks Country Club. He then wins Ali over by proclaiming himself a jerk, and it builds to that determined and somewhat over-the-top makeup kiss. When I asked John about how it should play out, he said, "Kiss like the kids do today." I was already nervous about it, due to my inexperience in this area on-screen. But what kind of direction is that? "Like the kids do"? It was all on me to represent what kids do today? Cue the pounding heartbeat and butterflies. *All right. Oh well, here goes. . . .* And there it went. When I look back at it, it's almost oddly fitting, for it mirrors many of the hairstyles and synthesized music of the era. A little heavy-handed and a bit much. So, in that sense, maybe it was like so many other moments in the *Karate Kid* universe . . . perfectly meant to be.

That scene was shot with the camera mounted on the end of a Chapman crane. The arm of the crane would rise up and follow Daniel and Ali onto the Golf N' Stuff parking lot in one continuous shot that revealed Daniel taking Ali over to show her the yellow '47 Ford convertible that Miyagi gave to him. This section has such relevance to me, as I remember reacting to a line pitch that John offered to me in the scene. When LaRusso hands the keys to Ali and says, "Here you go," she responds, surprised, with "You want me to drive?" The line John tossed out to me to respond with was:

"Hey, it's the eighties!"

I distinctly remember this as it happened. The line had me

cocking an eyebrow and made me think. I mean, I understood it, but I didn't understand it. At that point in my life, I would certainly never have come up with that line of dialogue myself. I was just twenty-two years old (yes, playing sixteen, and I promise I'll touch on that later). But I never looked at life in terms of decades. You know, like it's the fifties or it's the nineties or whatever. I was too young to use that reference in 1983. Or I wasn't even sure what decade I was in. I was just living life. However, I got what it meant. A guy would let the girl drive in the eighties, whereas that would not have been the case in an earlier generation. It struck me in the moment. For some reason it reverberated in my head as I was shooting the scene. What's mind-blowing to me now is how relevant it is today. I believe it was ahead of its time. And truthfully, it was a happy accident. I doubt John knew what "It's the eighties" would bring and how and where *The Karate Kid* would sit in that place in history. Just a reflective observation I wanted to share since I felt something I couldn't fully pinpoint on the day. It has stuck with me ever since. I remember saying that line as if it were yesterday.

I also remember laughing with Lisa and all the fun she had driving the convertible up and out of the parking lot. And the silliness of slow-dancing in the shower costume at the high school Halloween party before a raw egg was cracked over my head by a squawking kid in a chicken costume. I look back at Avildsen's posted YouTube videos of all of our rehearsals, and even then we were having fun. It's nice to see that.

But what happened to the Ali Mills character after the events of the original film was peculiar at best. It was not a good look in terms of how to treat that character, but I never really noticed it at the time. I became very busy with upcoming projects and it was not a focal point for me. I never called Lisa to discuss her feelings on this, something I believe I would handle differently if it happened today.

It felt like there was a show-*business* decision made to discontinue that character in the story going forward. Ali's character was written off in one measly line of dialogue at the top of the sequel, and the filmmakers decided to take the story in another direction with the Okinawa story line and Miyagi's family. They added a new LaRusso love interest and a new nemesis. As time has passed, I don't believe anyone thinks this was a respectful handling of the Ali character. Why was she not treated more appropriately? Fortunately, this was something we did have the opportunity to address in *Cobra Kai*, and I am really glad that we did. Jon, Josh, and Hayden, the creators of the show, were very sensitive to and respectful of Lisa's feelings when it came to honoring her character in the present-day story. And we addressed the deficiencies in how she was handled in the movie sequel. This was necessary, and the fans seemed to respond well to it. And I think for Lisa it gave her some closure after the awkward omission of her character, who deserved so much better at the time.

I ran into Lisa only once in all of the years between when we wrapped the first film and before we reunited on *Cobra Kai* in 2019. It was a brief encounter at a Mets World Series game at Shea Stadium in 1986. I had just finished up my Broadway debut in the stage play *Cuba and His Teddy Bear* with Robert De Niro. *Crossroads* had left the theaters, but *The Karate Kid Part II* was still playing on movie screens. I was in the thick of it and was not mindful of what Lisa's perspective probably was on the movie franchise that she had initially been a part of. Our encounter was in passing in the crowd right before the game started. It was tentative but friendly, and we went our separate ways to our seats. In that moment, I realized I should have been more cognizant of how it must have felt for her when her character was written out of the sequel.

The next time I saw her was on the stages of *Cobra Kai* in Atlanta, Georgia, in November 2019. The anticipation of her arrival was huge for the show. Everyone in the cast and on the crew was buzzing. The fan base had been begging for it. Ali was the character the show needed to have. The catalyst for the conflict between Daniel and Johnny all those years ago. And having Elisabeth Shue grace the series was massive for the show. But it was probably even more important for me than I knew . . . and I think for her as well.

There we were . . . thirty-three years later. Yes, it had been thirty-three years since I last saw Elisabeth Shue. Her résumé had been filled with many films and TV shows and a Best Actress Academy Award nomination since that first movie. What was I going to say? What would she have to say? The anticipation was building, as I knew it would. I am sure even more for her than me. There were decades to catch up on, so I was uncertain of how it would go. I only knew that my plan was to be welcoming and positive despite the unknown and our long absence from each other's careers and lives. And then the moment came. From around the corner, she approached, and I was there with one of our show's creators, Jon Hurwitz (a superfan of Ali Mills). He got to witness the reunion of Daniel and Ali first. Lisa and I locked eyes with a thousand thoughts racing in our heads, and in a split second she came out with "Oh my God!"

I found this surprising and hilarious and kind of weirdly appropriate. And I countered with "Oh my God? That's it? Who did you expect?" And we both laughed and embraced at the silliness of it, kind of covering our embarrassment that neither had something more eloquent to start with after all these years. There was just too much that had happened in all that time to try to tackle it in the first re-meeting. We have brought up this "OMG" moment a few times since, and it's always good for a smile and a great laugh.

We would spend the next few days filming and getting reacquainted in between scenes and sharing a bit of our lives' history since we'd last graced the screen together, and reminiscing about our connection to these characters and any missteps they might have made over the years. In the *Cobra Kai* script, we were able to address the "truth" of what happened in Daniel and Ali's breakup at the beginning of *Part II*. How there was a misunderstanding about Ali's UCLA friend whom

Daniel thought Ali had feelings for, and the accident she had with Mr. Miyagi's '47 Ford. Yes, that was the measly one-off line that carved Ali out of the movie franchise. The scene in *Cobra Kai* was playfully done over cocktails at a Christmas party, and there was finally some much-needed narrative closure there. And then there was our characters' goodbye scene, which seemed to mirror Ralph and Lisa as much as it served Daniel and Ali. A moment of nostalgia and earnest recognition when Daniel feels the need to apologize but Ali stops him short.

Lisa was wonderful in this scene. I think it surprised us, how emotional it became. How saying goodbye for the moment had all of the weight and acknowledgment of these two adored characters, the beloved adolescent darlings from *The Karate Kid,* and our connection to the world. And how we would always be linked through this movie and the magic that we'd created together. It was layered with reminiscence and bittersweet nostalgia. Embracing the present and saying goodbye to our youth all in the same moment. It was sweet and delicious. I was so happy to have it. By far my favorite moment of hers in the episode. I guess I would have to say it felt as satisfying and as fulfilling as a strawberry shortcake and a cannoli.

CHAPTER FOUR

———

The Zabka Experience

William (Billy) Zabka fast became the quintessential bad boy/villain in many eighties movies, such as *Just One of the Guys* and *Back to School*. But his first film role, the one that literally kicked it all off, was that of Johnny Lawrence in *The Karate Kid*. After filming the final fight sequence of the many fictitious beatdowns I took at the hands (and feet) of Mr. Zabka, I recall saying to myself, "Well, at least I don't have to ever deal with *that* guy again!"

Oh, young Skywalker, be careful what you wish for.

I had officially won the role of LaRusso at the point Billy and I had our first encounter. He didn't have to go through the screen test process like I did. He would be cast as Johnny off the videotaped audition he and I would do together for Avildsen. It was about a week or so after I had settled into my digs at the Beverly Comstock. I drove up and over the Santa Monica

Mountains into the Burbank area for another day of pre-production activities. On this particular day, the casting of Daniel's nemesis was a priority. I had parked my car in my assigned space on the Columbia Pictures studio lot and was approaching Bungalow One (the film's production office) when I first noticed Billy. There were a few Johnny Lawrence candidates hovering about nervously with their audition pages in hand. They were anxiously waiting to be called in to take their shot. Ron Thomas, who wound up playing Bobby in the film (another original Cobra Kai member), was also there trying out for the Johnny role, as were a few other blond contenders. It was like a golden boy convention. Each more studly and athletic-looking than the last. I imagined each with a customized surfboard on the top of a Jeep CJ-5 somewhere. At least that was my thought as I rounded the bend and made my way over to the bungalow.

They all seemed to perk up as I approached. I think they were eyeing me to get a feel for my reaction to them and possibly position themselves before getting in the room with Avildsen. This felt odd to me, as I was probably more nervous than they were. I knew that whoever became the chosen one was going to have a field day bullying me and kicking my ass for the better part of the next ten weeks. I remember reading the audition scene with one or two of them as we were waiting for John to show up. It's interesting when I think back; there was only one scene that was used in the Johnny auditions, and as it turned out, it was never in the movie. It was a scene in which Johnny approached Daniel with a form that needed to be signed before he competed in the All Valley tournament. It came late in the story and took place by the lockers at the high school. They each sized up the other and questioned the other's motives. It then escalated into an antagonistic standoff. The scene did have some defined layers, as it was one of the few "conversations" the two characters ever had in the script. That's why it was a good scene to audition with, but it wasn't the right exchange to have that late in the film itself. It took something away from the buildup to the tournament to have that aggressive an interaction right before the movie's climax. (This deleted scene is now featured in the extras on a newly released 4K Blu-ray box set of the original films.)

One interesting recollection to note was how sincere and friendly reading with my fellow thespians was when we practiced the scene in the parking lot beforehand. But oh, how that tune changed when we got in front of the director at showtime and the stakes were higher. Suddenly, I was being pushed and pulled. Fingers were pointed in my face. I felt forceful breath in my ear and spittle hitting my cheek. All the Johnnys were so amped up to show the director their worthiness. I, on the other hand, was receiving a wake-up call from the back-to-back berating. I began to see a snapshot of my filming life as Daniel LaRusso opposite Johnny Lawrence. *Strap in, Ralphie, it's going to be one hell of a ride.* If only I had known for how long.

There was something undeniably special and intense about Billy's energy and confidence level. I would have to describe his audition performance as all in. He had such a clear take on this role. I could tell Avildsen loved him for the part. He was the perfect Johnny Lawrence. When we got outside after the sessions were completed, Billy asked me how he had done in the audition. I remember saying to him, "I don't know for sure, man, but you scared the *shit* out of me!" And he did. He was intense and focused and intimidating and had a great look for this part. He responded to my account with a smirk that crept into a smile. I'm not sure if I remember his saying anything apologetic or particularly warming at the time. But I do remember that signature smirk. Like I said, he was the perfect Johnny Lawrence. And he still is.

Before we both knew it, we were thrust into martial arts training in preparation for all of our fight scenes, though at the outset we did not train together. Pat Johnson would train the Cobras separately from Miyagi and Daniel. The styles were polar opposites. Billy was training in an aggressive Korean fighting style called Tang Soo Do and I in the classic Okinawan Goju-Ryu soft style. But once we had reached a certain level of understanding and physical ability, Avildsen had Pat Johnson put us together to start designing the fight sequences. Pat then began instructing us on the choreography. Billy was instantly impressive. He had been a wrestler in high school and was a natural athlete. More recently, I was surprised to learn that he was born in New York and spent his first ten years living on Long Island just like me before he moved out west. His dad worked for NBC. I just assumed he was born and raised a quintessential California athlete. I never knew we had both been to New York Mets games as kids. You think you know a guy. . . .

It took Billy no time at all to turn into a martial artist. That was certainly my somewhat nervous impression at the time. *Oh shit, this guy's good at everything: kicking, punching, spinning, jumping . . . not to mention sweeping.* And I had to block it all with my scrawny forearms day after day after day. Fortunately, Billy was just as precise with his control as he was with his athletic ability. Well, for the most part. Story to come in a minute.

We rehearsed the fight sequences and action choreography virtually every single day during rehearsal, then again on set and in between scenes while we were making the film. It was the Avildsen mandate of "There's no such thing as being too good at it." Truth is, the majority of the quality time Billy and I spent together was when he was essentially kicking my ass! So the concept that at some point in our lives we would become accomplished acting partners and really good friends seemed very far from reality back then. While filming, I spent the lion's share of my time and days shooting scenes with Pat Morita, Lisa Shue, and Randee Heller, while for the most part, Billy spent his time with the Cobras and their evil sensei, Kreese.

Martin Kove, who played (and still plays) John Kreese, quickly became the Darth Vader of the eighties and the Thanos of 2022. He was cast late in the filmmaking process. I believe we were actually a few weeks into shooting before his role was set. At that time, Martin was on the TV series *Cagney & Lacey*, so I knew of him. We were never really very close during the making of the film. I mean, he was the dark villain teacher of my nemesis. There was no time for pleasantries with my packed shooting schedule. The less I interacted with "the bad guys," the more intimidating they were, and that all supported the end result on-screen.

Well, all of that has certainly changed in recent years. Marty as Kreese is still creating hurdles and problems for most every character in today's *Cobra Kai* series. He has quite the menacing presence in that role. But now we are such good friends off-screen and Martin Kove is just a teddy bear of a guy, a loving granddad and theatrical cowboy who fully embraces his sinister alter ego. I'm enjoying the reawakening of our characters today and the kinship that we now have off-screen. Marty and Billy have always been close since the completion of *The Karate Kid*. That was not the case with me at the time. I immediately jumped into production on the Nick Nolte movie *Teachers* right after we wrapped. My reconnection and current friendship with both of them came about many years later.

There was a day during the rehearsal time when Billy and the OG Cobras—Ron Thomas, Tony O'Dell, Chad McQueen, and Rob Garrison—played some soccer in between fight rehearsals. Pat Morita and I joined in for a bit. Not sure if Lisa was there, but I'm certain if she was, she would have left all of us in the dust. I mention this soccer memory because it was one of the few times, if not the only time, I interacted with the Cobras outside of the movie scenes, whether during rehearsal or filming. For the most part, Billy and the guys were "that part of the movie" to me. Meaning not the Miyagi side or family side, where so much of my acting focus was. The Cobra side usually consisted of getting tossed around and yelled at and hobbling away with a few bumps and bruises. So, despite how nice everyone was, I chose to come and go in that world without sticking around or overstaying my welcome.

The big fights with Billy consisted of the beach fight, the Halloween skeleton fight, and of course the finals of the All Valley tournament. We worked our asses off and it developed into such well-rehearsed precision. Avildsen would come often to videotape our progress and make any adjustments. Pat Johnson had us in padded gloves and forearm, knee, and shin pads as we started learning the choreography. Slowly we would shed them as the weeks went by. The fight sequences became second nature, downloaded fully into our brains and our bodies. It was like a ballet, or a tango, if you will. By the time we shot the big fight, we barely touched each other; that's how controlled we were. The success of this process spoke to Avildsen's diligent rehearsal plan, Pat Johnson's tutelage, and the execution of the dance by Zabka and Macchio—something we still talk about and are both so proud of.

There was one mishap in all of this perfection. It came to be in the wee hours of the morning. I'm thinking about four A.M. We were shooting nights. Our body clocks were still not quite fully calibrated to the graveyard shift of sleeping in daylight and working through darkness. The setting was the skeleton fight at the fence after the Halloween party. The five-on-one beatdown of LaRusso after he would not "leave well enough alone." This scene is one of the most iconic in the movie, a well-choreographed and exquisitely executed sequence by the cast and Pat Morita's fight double, Sensei Fumio Demura. Where the world discovers that Mr. Miyagi has a superpower and Daniel LaRusso has a new friend and mentor. But there was one behind-the-scenes blemish. When it happened, we were one roundhouse kick away from completing a flawless night of filming. Here's the theory of how and why it happened, and the way Billy and I still playfully debate it even to this day.

During an action sequence, when you change from a wide shot to a medium shot or from an over-the-shoulder to a close-up single, there are a few ways to do it. You can either move the camera, move the actors, or, if the camera has a zoom lens on it, just tighten the shot without moving the actors or the camera. Well, at four in the morning after a long night of fighting, the camera was on Billy as he was executing a roundhouse-type kick to my face. Somewhere between the over-my-shoulder shot on him, where his foot would wipe across my face (actually well in front of me), and the close-up shot of him, where his foot and leg would extend out of the camera's view—that was where the accident happened. I believe we moved the camera in closer to Billy and I was then positioned close to the lens off camera. But we never moved Billy's mark to adjust for the shorter distance. That's my story of how the night was over after take one of that specific camera angle. The kick wound up tagging me on the chin and pinballing my head off the side of the camera's matte box. G'night, everybody!

In retrospect, it could have been a lot worse. The end result was a stiff jaw for a few days and some minor bruising on my chin. Billy felt bad. He checked in on me as we were wrapping out and calling it a night to see how I was. He apologized— not that it was his fault; these things can happen. But I remember his joking about where the blame should fall for this "mishap," and always with that *smirk*. I am telling you, folks; he *is* the perfect Johnny Lawrence.

We still joke about it today. Very often we play it up at a Comic-Con panel or an interview and the fans love it. In the end, we consider it a draw or blame the unknown camera-crew member who didn't adjust the mark. All in all, with the amount of physical work we've done together, it's amazing how safe and injury-free we've been able to be. Practice, practice, practice does make (almost) perfect. He's a helluva fight partner. I just didn't know I'd still be squaring off with him in my late fifties!

As I mentioned earlier, Billy and I didn't stay in touch after the making of the movie, except during his character's return in the opening scene of *The Karate Kid Part II*. The scene picks up right after the tournament has ended. It takes place in the parking lot outside the arena. This initially was going to be the final scene in the original film. But they punted the scene because the filmmakers felt there was no place to go after the victory on the mat in the All Valley. You could not top that crane kick moment. The movie was over. It was determined then that this denouement scene in the parking lot between Miyagi and Kreese would be the perfect start to the sequel if it were to happen. They hedged their bets and it paid big-time dividends. *The Karate Kid Part II* was released in the summer of 1986 and took in an even bigger box office than the original. But for me and Billy, it was (temporarily) over. Except for the filming of that one scene in *Part II*, I wouldn't see him for roughly twenty years.

That changed in November 2005. I was bleary-eyed tired from not sleeping the night before, as I was preparing to speak at Pat Morita's funeral service in Las Vegas. I had a seven A.M. nonstop flight from New York, and the funeral service was that afternoon. The emotion of it all was fresh and consuming my mind as I was processing this reality. The pressure of what I wanted to say was mounting. It was a very difficult flight out to Vegas, and I was traveling alone. When I arrived at the service, I stayed pretty isolated at first and sat by myself. I attempted to go unnoticed until I felt ready to engage. I tentatively scanned the people in attendance until my eyes settled on Billy in one of the pews. He was there with Ron Thomas. Pat Johnson was next to them. Billy caught my gaze. He smiled and waved and I returned the same. No smirk, just a simple smile. It was warm and comforting to see him and Ron and Pat. There was a kindred-spirit connection, and it moved me. For the first time, after so many years of absence, I saw Billy from another perspective. It felt different. This time we were on the same side of the mat. We had separately come together to mourn our mutual friend. The fact that he was there to pay his respects to Pat meant something significant to me.

From that moment on it seemed we made it a point to stay in touch, and our friendship grew from there. We would catch up slowly but surely on the past twenty years at various Comic-Cons and screenings and panels that we would attend together. I learned that he was an Academy Award nominee for his short film *Most* in 2003. We shared an affinity for filmmaking, as I had made my short film *Love Thy Brother,* which premiered at Sundance in 2002. We were and still are very different; however, we share a common ground in those creative areas.

One day he called me about a parody music video he was going to direct and star in titled "Sweep the Leg," in which he would play a warped version of his Johnny Lawrence character living in a trailer park and not letting go of his past. He wanted to know if I would come on board and be involved, perhaps washing or waxing a car in one scene as a "cool cameo." It was a bit awkward, as at that time I was not even remotely ready to embrace that concept. Additionally, I was unsure of how it would turn out. He asked me if I would look at the rough cut when he was done with it and see what I thought. Well, I did, and it was terrific and funny with wonderful production values. I decided to participate and be the cameo button ending to the piece. It worked even better than what he originally pitched. And it was my first glimpse into Billy's interest in exploring these characters once again.

He would occasionally bring the point up to me over the next few years. He would say something like, "I think there's more story here." He had Marty on board to participate further as well. And the OG Cobras too. He was talking about an idea that could build to a potential "rematch." It was originally more in the comedic world, if my memory serves me. I never saw it or understood how to write it. I stood strong on my theory that we should leave the legacy untouched at that time unless I heard a brilliant idea or, even better, had something substantial to read and consider. For whatever reason, the conversations never evolved into someone putting pen to paper. Without actual material to judge, I wasn't willing to take a next step and get involved, officially, on any project connected to *The Karate Kid*. It was always easier (and safer) to say "No, thank you." I consistently stonewalled the idea of going back, even with the many pitches I had heard over the years. Nothing resonated with me. And no actual scripts or treatments materialized. They were mostly one-note ideas. I was very protective of the films and my character. What could we possibly improve? Pat Morita was no longer here. That vital element would be missing. The youthful face of Daniel LaRusso in that *hachimaki* headband, at that time and place, is woven into the fabric of the world. If whatever concept we went with missed the mark, that beloved legacy could be tarnished. That was my logic and I was at peace with it.

During that window of time, I did finally relent and play myself (not Daniel LaRusso) for the first time in an episode of HBO's *Entourage*. It was titled "Aquamansion" and turned out to be one of the most popular episodes of the entire series. It was funny and smart and proved to be the right call. Phew! You never know going in. Fans, critics, and showbiz industry folk all seemed to enjoy it. I mention this because when *How I Met Your Mother* approached both Billy and me to do an episode as ourselves, I initially felt, *Been there, done that*. Plus, the character was kind of written as window dressing, without a real purpose besides being Ralph Macchio at a bachelor party. So, I passed. Well, here's some advice. Don't tell your kids that their favorite show asked you on as a guest and you said no. They both came at me with "How dare you turn down *HIMYM*?! Who do you think you are, Dad?!" "Barney Stinson talks about *The Karate Kid* all the time." "That would be awesome!" *Okay, all right, okay, I'll reconsider.* So, I called Billy and learned that he had signed on and heard back from the writers of the series that they would incorporate my thoughts and collaborate on embellishing the Ralph Macchio character for that episode of the show. And the rest is prime-time comedy history. Once again, it proved to be the right call. Sometimes you just have to thank your kids.

What is significant about the turn in *HIMYM* is the focus on the William Zabka character's being Barney Stinson's hero. Neil Patrick Harris's character, Barney, insists Ralph Macchio played a punk kid from New Jersey who stole Johnny Lawrence's girlfriend and trophy with an illegal kick. And therein lies the seed of a concept that would grow and continue to resonate and ignite an ongoing debate. I will definitely be diving deeper into my feelings on this and other *Karate Kid* fan theories in a later chapter, but for now . . .

My journey with Mr. Zabka has been extraordinary. Who could have ever predicted our evolution from classic teen foes to adult friends and now screen partners in this global hit series? Not me, that's for sure. Today, we share a mutual feeling of protection concerning our characters and the film itself, yet from two distinctive viewpoints. Partnering up for *Cobra Kai* has given us a greater understanding of each other both as actors and as men. It has only become richer as we dive deeper. We have tons of fun with it all too, laughing about the silliness that these two fifty-plus-year-old guys allow their karate beliefs to dictate their lives' happiness and how the fans all love to be entertained by it. We discuss our hair-ology and the challenges of today versus the ease of yesterday. I mean, our eighties hair was abundantly awesome, amiright? We rib each other on our differences. We are vastly different both in and out of character. Avildsen got it right from the very start, as he did with every casting choice for *The Karate Kid*. He knew what instruments to put together to make the music. We just had no idea they would still be playing the songs and we'd be adding more verses today.

Aside from any differences, one of the similarities that Billy and I share is a keen eye for the cinematic homages to *The Karate Kid* within the storytelling of *Cobra Kai*. Jon, Josh, and Hayden are very mindful of this and do a beautiful job in keeping those homages and tones alive in the series. But often when you make a series for a world that watches a lot of its content on iPhones, specific visual details can get lost thanks to production pressures. You wind up catering to this generation born into close-ups and quick editing. It's a balance to keep the series' identity defined yet embrace the movie's signature as well. The film had numerous scenes that would play out in one continuous shot, allowing the action to unfold and breathe organically. Often that requires a good deal of rehearsing to have the scene in "show shape" before the cameras roll. This was something we did a lot on the film with Avildsen at the helm but often do not have the production time to achieve in *Cobra Kai*.

There are a few examples I could share, but there's one in particular with Billy where we were rehearsing a scene with a group of actors. It had movement to it, and individual camera angles were being planned to cover everyone's action and dialogue. Right before we were about to shoot the master (the wider camera angle before you move in with tighter shots to get "coverage"), I looked to Billy and one of us said, "Why are we breaking up the flow and covering this?" I'm not sure if it was me or him who said it or if it happened simultaneously. We reminded each other how we would have shot this had it been in the *Karate Kid* film. We decided to present this idea to the episode's director and the show's producers. We all agreed to rework the blocking and movement so we could capture it all in one fluid shot. In fairness, there have been some spectacular *Cobra Kai* "oners," single-shot fight sequences that were designed to be filmed in one long take, but this example specifically pertains to a dialogue scene. It worked extremely well, and through this very simple example, I hope I've shown how gratifying it was to collaborate with Billy on yet another moment that threw back to the creative vision that got us here. It felt warm and fulfilling. I imagined that was Avildsen shining down on his boys like the sun.

I can't begin to explain the tandem joy Billy and I share about expanding *The Karate Kid*'s legacy and its relevance with the success of *Cobra Kai*. Whether it's a *Good Morning America* interview or a magazine photo shoot or Billy going up to snag and save my high-and-outside ceremonial first pitch at the start of a New York Mets game, we have been thrust into a connected partnership, one that we do not take for granted. Many people have asked me, "How did you know Zabka could deliver on *Cobra Kai*?" "Who would have thought you guys would be so good together?" And yes, that was a bit of an unknown going in. Would we be too overeager or attempt to hit a five-run homer every time we stepped up to the plate? Would all of the dry years as scarcely employed actors add up to his or my trying too hard and not playing the nuances?

My answer to these questions lives in my theory that there is a confidence in our understanding of these characters and the shoes that only we have walked in. We both approach our portrayals with great care and respect for the work we did back in 1983 and our admiration of that experience. The association with the legacy of *The Karate Kid* is one that we own and trust with our instincts. This is taking nothing away from the brilliant writing and vision of Jon, Josh, and Hayden and their team, without whom we would *not* have this current success. But there is an otherworldliness to the blessings of our little-movie-that-could that almost can't be fully explained. Billy and I speak of that all the time. How this franchise has been "kissed" in some way from the start. I will elaborate later on the pinpoint moment from the set of *Cobra Kai* when it all became crystal clear to us both. When we realized that our dynamic together had even more gravity than we knew. Something special seems to happen whenever "LawRusso" inhabits the *Cobra Kai* story. The experience of working with Billy has grown deeper and richer as the pages have turned. But no example may be more significant than the moment everyone had been waiting for . . .

From the earliest announcement of the *Cobra Kai* series, much attention had been paid to the concept of a long-awaited

"*Karate Kid* rematch." Over the first three seasons, there had been little nuggets placed throughout episodes teasing the inevitable showdown between our characters. When and how would it play out? And who would win? The excitement was building as the question of who would prevail hung out there for all to debate.

Well, it finally did happen in episode 5, season 4. After thirty-seven years of deliberation, Zabka and Macchio strapped on their respective *gi*s and hit the mat for what some have labeled "the most anticipated rematch in movie history."

During pre-production, everyone involved felt the pressure to deliver on this premier showcase. The writers certainly had to plan it perfectly, and at the right time in the arc of the series' story. Our martial arts choreographer, Don Lee (carrying the torch of the great Pat Johnson from the original film franchise), along with the stunt team had to design the three-point contest to reflect the two opposing fight styles. The goal was to pay tribute to the original film's iconic match yet create a new spectacle that would serve the current series.

For me (and I know for Billy as well), our focus was on respecting the characters—not solely on a "big fight" that would be primarily fan service. The *Cobra Kai* creators are always dedicated to that as well in both their writing and story execution. The stakes needed to be high, and they were. Bottom line: The winner of the match would gain sole possession of the reins and train the students in their fighting style, with the other having to stand down and accept it.

Billy and I spoke early on. We didn't want to chase the past and attempt a redo of what had been done when we were so much younger. It was important for us to allow Daniel and Johnny to be true to their age and to embrace that honestly. We had a little more prep time than usual to get ready for the big day, a bit reminiscent of our rehearsals when making the original film. We carefully thought through all of the beats and broke them down in detail from each perspective. It was the yin and yang of Johnny and Daniel as much as Billy and Ralph. We complemented each other as we worked to build the sequence from the ground up, not just physically but mentally and emotionally as well. In 1984, they were two kids trying to win a trophy for their senseis. In 2021, they were two men fighting for their beliefs, overshadowed by their stubbornness.

And there we were . . . on the mat. It was yesterday all over again—despite the occasional creaking knee or tight hamstring. (It's all about the stretching these days, folks!) We rehearsed hard and were dialed in for two nights of filming out in the cold and under the lights. The guidance and support from the *Cobra Kai* stunt team was impeccable. It all went exceptionally well (no roundhouse mishaps), and the contest was tagged with a humorous end beat to keep the verdict unresolved. Neither character walked away with any bragging rights, and that was just pitch-perfect from the *Cobra Kai* writers' room.

Aside from our frozen toes from what were unseasonably cold winter nights in Atlanta, the scene was fresh and exciting, and it more than met expectations. There was one point while filming when Billy and I had wondered what the ticket prices would have been if it was a public event. We laughed out loud at the concept. Who knows? I'm sure the hard-core fans would have loved a pay-per-view live event. And we chuckled some more at the amusement of it all. Both of us were proud of what was accomplished. What a thrill it was to play in *The Karate Kid* sandbox once again. Partners in battle in the name of entertainment. And it all led to yet another Daniel and Johnny breakup at the conclusion of the episode. Of course it did.

So, what does the future hold for both Daniel LaRusso and Johnny Lawrence? What happens to these two beloved characters going forward? The fans long for them to somehow work together, yet they thoroughly enjoy themselves when they are at each other's throats. I often describe this area as the "Ross and Rachel" of our show. Keeping the rivalry alive while offering a taste of the two characters united is critical to the longevity. Making sure that ball stays up in the air is both challenging and creatively fulfilling. But as the show expands and the ensemble grows, there is less exclusive emphasis on the Daniel-and-Johnny of it all. This is despite the fact that they will always be the central pillars of the series.

There is still plenty of meat left on the bones of these guys. Furthermore, how they affect the next generation of "Karate

Kids" only adds to the possibility of a long, continuing story, if not solely in *Cobra Kai*, then perhaps in another extended arm of the *Karate Kid* universe. The possibilities may be endless. And if I'm ever asked how long we would like to keep this going and continue playing these characters, I'll say this, as emphatically as Zabka delivered it in 1984 . . .

"We'll decide when we've had enough, man!"

CHAPTER FIVE

The Crane Takes Flight

I have learned that throughout Asia, the crane is a symbol of happiness and eternal youth. In Japan, the bird is considered a mystical or holy creature. It symbolizes good fortune and longevity because of its fabled life span of a thousand years. With that, I have personally accepted the good fortune of forever being linked to the crane in cinema and pop culture. Why not be associated with happiness, longevity, and eternal youth, right? Sign me up! The belief that good things to come may be associated with this species of bird lends itself to understanding yet another insightful piece of the *Karate Kid* puzzle. However, when it came to the crane *kick* itself, I will offer a favorite Miyagi-ism.

"Not everything is as seem."

It's interesting when I think back to the origin of the crane kick—or at least the first time I read about it in Robert Kamen's script. It worked so well on paper and paid off beautifully on the page. But in actual, practical reality, it was not so easy to achieve. As a matter of fact, it was essentially impossible to pull off. I once read an interview with Kamen, who was asked about the crane technique and the basis of it. Robert's response was, "I made it up. It was just something I thought up on the spot. You have no balance. Your hands aren't in a defensive position. It's just cinematic."

Yes, this is true. He did make it up. It was cinematic. And at first, it was perfectly impossible to execute from script to screen. Seasoned stuntmen and martial artists all gave it their best shot. But as I recall, the kick conceived in the script just wasn't working no matter what we did. I eventually thought, *Uh-oh, this crane thing might not work!*

On paper it was described as Daniel LaRusso balancing on one leg (the other being the injured leg that was swept in a previous match). Then, with the base leg he is standing on, he throws a high front snap kick and lands back on that good leg he just kicked with. The injured leg would never touch the ground. Made sense, right? However, we soon learned that to pull off the maneuver seamlessly, one would have to switch base legs after the kick was snapped and then quickly switch back to standing on the healthy leg. The kick lost its fluidity whenever someone tried it with only one leg engaged and having to do all of the work. No one could effectively stick the landing without seeming off-balance. If I remember correctly, there was even talk of doing it with wires to achieve the height necessary to throw the kick with enough time to return the good leg to the base position for landing.

The problem was eventually solved by an acrobatic martial artist by the name of Darryl Vidal. Darryl appears in the movie as Johnny Lawrence's semifinals opponent. He was the person who figured out the best way to execute the move, transferring his weight effortlessly to fulfill the cinematic promise of what Kamen intended. Darryl was a spectacular aerial martial artist, almost balletic in his fluidity. The Baryshnikov of karate. His ability and technique created a seamless move and the blueprint for what Daniel-san needed to achieve. He also doubled for Pat Morita (with body padding and bald cap), specifically when Mr. Miyagi is on the log at the beach where Daniel first sees the crane technique in the distance.

I was dedicated and put in the training hours with both Darryl and Pat Johnson to learn the technique. In the end, it was modified into the magic trick that won the All Valley final match. I worked my butt off to master the move as best I could. I was determined not to succumb to a stunt double having to do it for me. That was not an option in my mind. Avildsen and Kamen seemed impressed with the hard work and end result. And my fight partner, Billy Zabka, impressively sold the impact on the B-side to my A-side. It was a tag-team moment. A synchronized execution, with Billy's taking the hit equally as important as my delivering the kick. It played out in a low and wide shot with no smoke or mirrors or special effects. Just a perfectly placed camera angle that made it heroic and celebratory. I am sure if we counted all of the takes, they would add up to at least thirty times of us running the crane kick sequence. I don't recall ever tiring of doing it over and over during the shooting day. The adrenaline of the moment and the personal achievement seemed to carry me through. I was extremely proud of it. We shot it from multiple angles as well, sometimes in slow motion, sometimes super close for impact.

Those shots were never used in *The Karate Kid*. Only the low, wide angle. That other footage went unseen until *Cobra Kai*. The creators of the series were able to access the archives of the Sony/Columbia Pictures film vault and use camera angles never edited into the original movie for *Cobra Kai*. It's interesting to note that when we used close-ups and slow-motion versions of the kick in the TV series, it altered the perspective. You felt the impact to Billy's character because the camera angle was not focused on the cinematic beauty of the crane technique itself. For the moment, you sympathized with Johnny Lawrence as he got kicked, and that setup worked for the initial concept of *Cobra Kai*. In *The Karate Kid* itself, the moment was all about the victory for Daniel LaRusso and Mr. Miyagi's magic. The bully got his comeuppance. The crowd jumped to their feet cheering for their hero. Euphoria. To the victor went the spoils. Something iconic was born on that shooting day. But I still never expected that crane kick to catapult the movie's climax into the stratosphere the way it did.

———

U sing the most famous kick in cinematic history as metaphor, the same would be true with the release of our little movie in the summer of 1984. I say "little movie," as I am referencing it in comparison to all the big-budget releases that surrounded it that year. It was the beginning of the supernatural era of blockbusters. What were the odds that we would cut through all of that noise and not get drowned out in the sea of special-effect event movies? Two weeks prior to *The Karate Kid*'s release, both *Ghostbusters* and *Gremlins* were leading the box office. *Indiana Jones and the Temple of Doom*, a leftover from May, was still a powerhouse and hot ticket. And right there in the middle of all these tall skyscrapers was this charming town house with a warm fireplace that made everyone feel good. *The Karate Kid*, released in June, became a summertime sleeper hit that was still playing in theaters deep into the fall.

The film worked; we knew that pretty quickly. It was well received by most critics. But who knew it would gain that kind of traction with the audience and continue building wider from there? Word of mouth started to spread, and *The Karate Kid* became the alternative movie for all ages. It developed into must-see entertainment. Friends would tell friends, and uncles would tell cousins, and kids would tell parents. The lines would grow longer and longer, and before I knew it the crane stance had become commonplace in the schoolyard and certainly at the beach. Waxing on and off would be a normal reference at the car wash. And at beauty salons, for that matter, as well. It was the beginning of the groundswell, and it was fascinating and kind of unbelievable to be on the inside of it watching it unfold.

I wonder if it would be different nowadays. Back then, especially in the summertime, movies were king. Those were the plans you made. "What do you want to see?" "Yeah, we're meeting up at the movies." "I'm dying to see this." "Let's go again!" There weren't a zillion things to watch on your phone or daily content on YouTube. No Netflix or Hulu for on-demand viewing. Even many of the cable channels didn't exist during that time. I'm curious whether the film's rapid ascent was due to those reasons. If you weren't at the beach or in the pool, then you were at the movies. Sure, today you have social media to instantaneously share information and get the word out, but there is just so much more content. So many more pieces of information in so many different categories. Back in the day there was less to consume and less to be consumed with. The larger word-of-mouth stories were not clouded and cluttered by the onslaught of special interests and subcategories. So, perhaps that is why *The Karate Kid* felt so present on the street and in the malls and supermarkets. Or maybe it was the fact that *I* was that Karate Kid these folks were speaking of, so it was all sort of spotlighted for me. Yeah, that's probably it. Regardless, it was the game-changing summer of 1984, and my life moved into overdrive.

My attention was split among so many areas. I had one foot in my home life and one foot in my getting-more-recognized actor life. The New York Mets were having a solid season and their rookie right-handed flamethrower Dwight Gooden was the talk of the town. Any chance I could get to see him pitch at Shea Stadium was something I took advantage of. There was an excitement and buzz in the air that is not often witnessed. He won Rookie of the Year in '84 and his stuff was electric. It was thunder at the ballpark every called third strike, with the batter's knees buckling at the plate as the ball popped into the catcher's glove. At the same time, Bruce Springsteen was on his *Born in the USA* tour with the E Street Band. They played ten shows in New Jersey at the Brendan Byrne Arena. I was at four of them, including the first and last, on August 5 and August 20, epic, marathon concerts I will never forget.

For the most part, when I went out, I'd have a hat on and a pair of cheap drugstore sunglasses. Ray-Ban knockoffs and a Mets hat were that summer's look. But it often didn't work. At the games, concerts, or restaurants, people would call out their favorite phrase from the movie or assume their awkward crane stance. I would smile and high-five, and it was always friendly. For whatever reason, I felt far more like a local hero and much less like a movie star. I was treated like the guy who won the high school football game on a Friday night. The kid who lived next door. Not a celebrity you would see on the red carpet or in magazines. Even though sometimes I was. I believe some of this was due to my openness in how I interacted with people. But a lot of it had to do with Daniel LaRusso and his approachability as a character. He was "one of our own". . . and I think I was too. And here is where the lines get blurred.

After Springsteen had left town on his tour and the Mets were accelerating toward a pennant race (the Cubs beat them out that year, but in '86 they took the World Series), I was alerted that Columbia Pictures would be sending me to Europe in September for a few international press events for openings of *The Karate Kid*. The whirlwind press tour concluded at the Deauville American Film Festival in France. Before that I had stops in London, England; Hamburg, Germany; and Stockholm, Sweden. When you visit these countries with a movie opening, you are treated incredibly well. Everyone goes out of their way to pamper you with nice hotels and fancy meals and gift baskets. I enjoyed the praise and attention, but the back-to-back press interviews and crowded itineraries had me missing my hometown digs and peeps. I had maybe two or three days in each place with little leisure time for exploration. This was mainly a work trip.

I specifically recall something quite humbling that happened as I exited the plane in Stockholm. I had already been to England and Germany by this point and had my eyes on the final stop in France. As I got off the plane and made my way through the Jetway toward the terminal, I began to hear crowd noise building. When I crossed through the doorway that opened up into the gate area, it was packed with people. At least a hundred fans with flowers and balloons, camera strobes flashing. I was overwhelmed. *Wow, I am huge in Sweden. Who knew?* Well, this rush of unexpected excitement quickly deflated when I turned and realized Björn Borg was standing right behind me waving to the people of his home country. The world-famous tennis player (eleven-time Grand Slam singles champion) apparently had been right behind me the whole flight, and I'd never noticed. That was far more frustrating than misunderstanding the fans' cheers. I was a massive Borg fan. I'd watched all of his marathon matches against Jimmy Connors and John McEnroe. Sadly, I never got the chance to say hello as he was swept away by his reps with the crowd cheering throughout the terminal. Then, suddenly, it became eerily quiet as I looked around for the lone Columbia Pictures international rep who would escort me through customs. It was a solid reality check for my young ego. I brushed it off with a smile and a head shake as I moved into my day of Swedish Q and As on the adventures of Daniel LaRusso.

When I arrived in France at the Deauville American Film Festival, there was an enormous banner hanging on one of the buildings displaying the words *Le Moment de Verité*. It was essentially a version of the familiar *Karate Kid* poster; however, the title had been changed. Its English translation was "The Moment of Truth." I was surprised that they would elect not to do a literal translation of the actual title of the film, as silly as I had always thought it was. Why change it now? It seemed to be settling in as the film's popularity grew. Well, apparently this alternate title was applied in a few countries. Mainly the territories of the world where karate was not popular or where it possibly had a negative connotation. This was a calculated marketing decision made by the studio. "The Moment of Truth" was also the name of the song that played under the film's end credits. The band Survivor had had a big hit with "Eye of the Tiger" for *Rocky III*, so they were brought in to create a song for our film. Bill Conti (the film score composer) collaborated on the music, and the song and title were born. As with so many callbacks to the *Karate Kid* universe, the *Cobra Kai* creators presented the reimagining of that song once again in the *Cobra Kai* series when Carrie Underwood made an appearance in the Netflix show. She rocked a new version during the All Valley Karate Championship, underscoring a montage that led to the climax of season 4.

When I returned home from Europe at the end of September 1984, the leaves were noticeably beginning to turn and autumn was in the air. The film was still playing in theaters, and I could feel its presence out on the street and, more pointedly, at one of my favorite Japanese restaurants.

Since the making of the film, and my accepting some of Pat Morita's tutelage, I had become more adventurous in my sushi choices, though I imagine any hard-core foodies would still have labeled me as conservative by comparison. I also had become far more proficient with chopsticks. That would prove to present an invitation for anyone in the restaurant to go in for the joke—to search for any flying insect and call out the question "Hey, Ralph, can you come over here and catch this for us?" Hahaha! I learned to roll with it and humor them with a smile. Once a busboy asked if I could instruct him on cleaning the table properly: "Is it left-hand circle or right-hand circle?" These jokes were often followed by, "Do those moves really work?" or "How did you do that fly-catching scene?" I told an abbreviated version of the story of the fly-catching scene on *The Tonight Show* in 2018. It killed. The audience and Jimmy Fallon loved it. The recollection inspires me to elaborate further and share it with you now.

With today's CGI technology, shooting the fly-catching scene would be a breeze. The fly would be added in postproduction and I would have just imagined it there on the day and reacted to it. But in 1983, we attempted to shoot it "practically." And when I say "attempted," I mean "attempted." It took lots of planning and a few days to conclude that this was another example of the fact that *not everything is as seem.* The tools we used to attempt this cinematic feat were two sets of chopsticks, one roll of extremely thin monofilament fishing line, one six-foot square pipe frame, one bamboo stick, some glue, three fake flies, and six to eight live ones. Okay, here's how it went.

First attempt: We attached a small plastic fly to one end of a piece of fishing line and the other end to the bamboo stick. A prop guy and/or first assistant director dangled it in front of me as I attempted to capture the fake fly with my chopsticks. This failed to work, as the fly looked artificial and appeared to be bouncing and not actually flying. No good.

Second attempt: The prop team secured a taut piece of fishing line across the pipe frame and glued a fake fly to the line at the midpoint. Two crew guys would hold the frame on either side, off camera, attempting to move the tethered fake fly in a more fluid manner. When I endeavored to "catch" that specific fly, it would snap the taut fishing line, rendering this concept unworkable. Next.

Third attempt: Glue a smaller fake fly to one side of one chopstick. Keep the fly from camera's view at first. Then quickly twist the chopstick at precisely the right moment while bringing the second chopstick down on the fly simultaneously. I would then act like I'd just snagged the fly out of thin air. If memory serves, I broke off the plastic fly and it fell to the table, and it was never convincing, as the fly appeared to come out of nowhere. Time to dust off and go with plan D.

Fourth attempt: It turned out our on-set still photographer was a whiz at catching flies with his bare hands. We figured, let's go with the real deal! This is gonna be it! He would trap a fly in his hands. Somehow, he'd be able to steady it so the prop guy could lasso the fly with the fishing line around its "neck." (Not sure flies have necks, but anyway . . .) Essentially, we made a flying leash, if you will. Now, this looked very real, as the fly could still fly around but it would not go out of the general area as it was secured to the line, which was held at the other end by the prop guy. Problem was, every time I would grab at the line with my chopsticks and slide down to the live fly, it wound up decapitated from the force. Fly bodies and fly heads went everywhere. It was a massacre I'm not very proud of. Additionally, the longer the fly was attached to the fishing line, the more tired it became; the weight of the line on these poor little guys proved to be too much, and they'd expire mid-take. A sad day in Hollywood . . . yes it was.

Fifth and final attempt: The next day the creative minds all put their heads together and decided, "Let's shoot it in reverse." What?! Well, that's exactly what we "attempted" to do. I would start with a live fly on a leash and put it in between the chopsticks (carefully trying not to crush it yet still holding it in place). Then we'd roll cameras. I'd start out smiling and excited about having caught the fly. I'd hold this jubilation a significant beat before *acting backward* by letting it go and moving my eyes and chopsticks around as if I were trying to locate the fly and dial in to grab it with said chopsticks. I would pay money to have this footage today. It was hideous and did not work on any level. An epic failure that kept me from adding "backward acting" to my résumé under *Special*

Talents. Oh well. In the end, I believe we wound up using a combination of the live fly on the fishing line and the tiniest plastic fly glued to the chopsticks. Through the magic of fine film editing, they created the illusion that it actually happened. And there you have it. The power of suggestion wins again!

Whether it was because of the fine-tuning of the crane technique or the Miyagi wisdom that "man who catch fly with chopstick accomplish anything," *The Karate Kid* was securing its place amid the heavy hitters of that time period. Robert Kamen's script under the direction of John Avildsen had struck a chord, and the harmony was reverberating into every area of my life. I remember sometime around Thanksgiving, I had gotten word that Jerry Weintraub's prediction that we'd make "a couple of these" was about to come true. Columbia Pictures was set to pick up my option for a sequel to the original film. *The Karate Kid Part II* would be on the way. At the same time, I was circling *Crossroads* as another film I wanted to do. Fortunately, it was a Columbia Pictures property as well, so we were able to manipulate the schedules so I could do both. In preparation, I was studying all facets of blues guitar and retraining in martial arts simultaneously. In 1985 I filmed *Crossroads* and *The Karate Kid Part II* back-to-back without a break, my busiest career year to that point.

The crane was taking flight and beginning to carve its place in American cinema and popular culture. Its profound influence on my life had begun to take shape. I just never anticipated the good fortune and longevity associated with this mystical bird would be cast upon me too.

As far as the eternal youth part? . . . I'm working on it!

CHAPTER SIX

The "Eighties" of It All

One of the things I hear most when fans reference *Cobra Kai* on Netflix is how much they love the nostalgia that is woven into the series, the undeniable homage to the eighties. That movie era has become a favorite for so many. The music. The dating scenes. The heroes and villains. The kick-ass training montages. Not to mention the big hair and the mismatched outfits. Who can forget LaRusso in his camouflage pants and tucked-in plaid shirt? No belt, of course.

When I am asked what I remember most about the eighties—the outfits, the music, the movies, the fads, the TV shows, or the catchphrases—I really don't come back with a quick answer or one that is particularly well versed on the era. For me, at the time, I was on the outside of it. Or, more accurately, on the way-way inside of it. I find it funny and notable that I have less knowledge of that time period than most. I was fairly out of touch about what was cool or trendy, as I was honestly living in a bubble. My experience was different from that of those who were out and about. I was kind of going from movie set to movie set during those years. And when I was on location and not filming, I was in either my rented apartment or my hotel room, prepping for my next day of work. I remember Rob Lowe joking that I should have a T-shirt that said "Do Not Disturb" on the front. That was often the sign on my hotel room doorknob during *The Outsiders*. And up to that point, when I wasn't working, I was usually back home on Long Island, lying pretty low there as well. Perhaps that's why I never got sucked in to all the partying and the drugs that were flowing so freely during that era—an observation that I will circle back to later in the book.

This chapter is less about chronicling the big events of that time and more a personal perspective based on my own experience, with the addition of a story or two to set some records straight. After all, I never got a Brat Pack membership card or even an invitation to join. So, what do I really know about the eighties of it all? That being said, Daniel LaRusso *is* a Chia Pet these days, so I must know something worthwhile about the era. Even if I was never asked to be in a John Hughes movie. Well, I did get close . . . once.

It was after the filming of *The Outsiders*. I was in Los Angeles. At that time Emilio Estevez and I would hang out on occasion. I even stayed over at his house once or twice, as it was in the Malibu area and it was a pretty long drive back to whatever hotel I might have been staying at. I recall at least once staying in his brother Charlie's room when he was either out of town or out for the night. This was in late '82 or early '83 and before *The Karate Kid* happened. I remember both Emilio's agent and my agent securing us each appointment times to audition for John Hughes for his new Universal Pictures coming-of-age movie *Sixteen Candles*. Emilio was to audition for the studly handsome guy, and I was being seen for the geeky-nerd kid. I'm a little unclear on whether it was his idea, mine, or both, but we thought it would be cool to audition together. This is something that is not customary on the first round. The casting folks and directors usually like to focus on one actor at a time, and then in further audition rounds they might bring people together for a chemistry read. But I think since Mr. Hughes and the casting team knew that Emilio and I had just completed a film together, they allowed us to come in and read at the same time. As a side note, the previous year, Francis Ford Coppola had had a lot of us actors reading and auditioning together for *The Outsiders*. Perhaps that info had traveled around town in Hollywood and it became something more openly accepted at the outset in casting sessions. In any event, Emilio and I were granted approval to go to the Universal Studios lot and tag-team our presentation of the audition material for John Hughes's *Sixteen Candles*.

We didn't receive any specific coaching or instructions. We only had the general breakdown of the characters and probably the latest draft of the script. He and I just sort of worked out our own version of the scene and added our own blocking and interpretations. Since it was laced with teen antics and comedy, we were looking to highlight the jokes. I came up with a certain nerdy walk for the character and a geeky nasal voice that I chose to speak with. I felt pretty confident, if not cocky, going in, and it took the edge off any nerves having a fellow ex-greaser alongside me. But needless to say, neither of us got our respective parts. The one thing I do recall most vividly is that after each take, Mr. Hughes would make an attempt to instruct me to dial down the character-y-ness a bit. I would say to myself, *But this guy is a super-nerd, a total geek. I have to layer that on at least a little bit.* Then, after my second failed attempt to win him over, the casting director took me aside and walked me out of the room. He instructed me to take a minute and just come back in as myself and read the scene simply. I recall the words "We just want natural Ralph, that would be perfect. You don't need to put any spin on it."

Nevertheless, my final attempt was still unsuccessful in stripping away the nerd-play that I was determined to infuse into this audition piece. Clearly, I didn't take the direction fully to heart, or maybe, just maybe (and more likely), it bruised my ego to hear that I could be convincing as this geek without even trying. Yep, that was it. I was too cool in my own mind. I have always found this story amusing in retrospect and wondered whether that indeed is what killed any chance for me to ever have an opportunity to work on a John Hughes movie. I doubt that is really the case, but it still makes me wonder what if. I shared the story with Anthony Michael Hall (who won the role, which launched his career) decades later at

Family cruise in '76 with Mom, Dad, and Steven. The matching shirts.

First grade.
Bow tie was a must in school pics.

Wasn't kidding.
I wanted to be Gene Kelly.

High school graduation pic.
Bow tie grew to enormous
and velvet in '79.

Young love.
With Phyllis between *The Outsiders* and *The Karate Kid*.

It's official: I got the part!

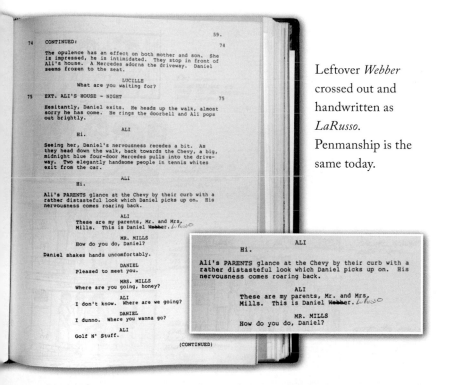

Leftover *Webber* crossed out and handwritten as *LaRusso*. Penmanship is the same today.

John Avildsen's storyboard. A rehearsal "accident" that became a little moment in the movie.

Preproduction rehearsal itinerary.

PAN WITH ALI & DANIEL AS THEY GO TO GREET HER PARENTS—

SC—75

ALI & DANIEL TO PARENTS— DANIEL PLEASED TO MEET YOU

SC—75

CUT TO LOW SHOT FULL FIG. IN FRAME AS THEY SHAKE HANDS—

SC—75

DANIEL NERVOUSLY KNOCKS OUT A LOOSE BRICK ON PARENTS FRONT PORCH—

SC—75

SCHEDULE

TUES. OCT. 11,1983

Morning   John A. with   BMX and Teacher.

1:00PM   John A., Alan F.,Pat J., and Sam G. for Truck With Bottles

2:ooPM   John A. with Pat J. in gym (Stg.15) with Stunt Dbl.
           for Ralph (Sc.115)

4:00PM   John A. With Pat J. in Stg. 15 Gym with: Fumio Demura,
           and Gerald Okamura (Stnt. Dbls For Miyagi). Pat
           Morita to attend.

5P - 6P   John A. with R. Bruno & A. Swinson RE: Wardrobe

WED. Oct. 12, 1983

7:30AM   John A., Cliff C. and Richard D. Location scout of
           Birmingham High School (Corner of Victory & Balboa)

7:45AM   John A., Cliff C., Richard D.,Alan O., Pat J., Alan F.
           Hope G., Sammy G. Leave School for Rehearsal at
           Lake Chatsworth.

10:00AM   Ralph M., Pat M. leave from bungalow 1 for Lake
           Chatsworth.

4:00PM   Cliff C., Alan F., Bill Z., Robert S. G.,Chad McQ.,
           "Bobby", Cobra #1, Meet at Bungalow 1 for Motorcycle
           work (At the Columbia Ranch).(Alan O. to Participate)

THURS. Oct. 13,1983

10:00AM   John A., Pat M., Ralph M., Cliff C., Pat J., and
           Hashimoto, with Sammy G. rehearse in Gym (Stg. 15)
           (Sammy will show some bonsai trees also)

2:00PM   John A., Cliff C., Pat J., Ralph M., Pat M., Bill Z.,
           Bill Conti, James Crabe for Karate Revue (all
           Karate Choreography to date)

4:30PM   John A., Cliff C., Hope R., Richard B., Aida S.,
           Lisa S., Two groups of Cheerleaders Audition at the Ranch

5:00PM   John A., Cliff C., Hope G.,Ralph M., Bill Z., Robert G.,
           "Bobby",Two Soccer Teams for try outs at Columbia Ranch.

11-12:30P Ralph M., Lisa S., and Rildo N soccer practice at the
           Ranch.

Handwritten call sheet.

On-the-job training. My film school.

Avildsen frames the kid.

Wait, what?!

Staying sharp in between scenes.

Lesson One from the Master.

BTS with
Randee Heller.
Friends and family.

Daniel and Ali.

All smiles with John and Lisa Shue making the "Ali with an I" scene.

Pat Morita's tour de force: the Miyagi drunk scene.

How is *that* not illegal, Mr. Lawrence?!

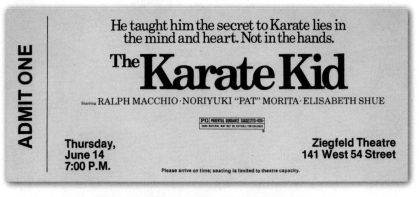

He taught him the secret to Karate lies in
the mind and heart. Not in the hands.

The **Karate Kid**

Starring RALPH MACCHIO · NORIYUKI "PAT" MORITA · ELISABETH SHUE

PG PARENTAL GUIDANCE SUGGESTED
SOME MATERIAL MAY NOT BE SUITABLE FOR CHILDREN

Thursday,
June 14
7:00 P.M.

Please arrive on time; seating is limited to theatre capacity.

Ziegfeld Theatre
141 West 54 Street

Official press preview ticket.

Ah, the '80s! With Phyllis at the premiere of *Great Balls of Fire!*

COURTESY OF RON GALELLA/GETTY IMAGES

"If it ain't on the page, it ain't on the stage." *The Karate Kid* creator,
Robert Kamen, with Pat and me on *Part II*.

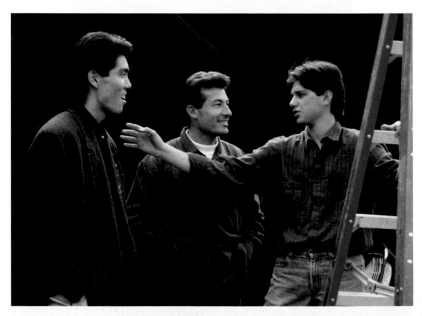

Yugi Okumoto visits the set of *Part III*,
here with my longtime friend Stan Rodarte (my stand-in).

A toast from Pat. (LEFT TO RIGHT: producers R J Louis and Jerry
Weintraub, myself, John Avildsen, and cinematographer James Crabe)

It was quite the partnership.

Asian Excellence Awards in NYC.
A perfect evening for our last time together.

COURTESY OF TAI MONG

Been with me since December '83.
Trophy was a wrap gift. I pocketed the
headband for myself. Who knew?

Times Square in NYC with two OGs:
Billy Zabka and that '47 Ford. *Cobra Kai* Season 2 promo.

Martinis, steaks, and Kamen's cab. Billy and I toast with the *Cobra Kai* series creators. (LEFT TO RIGHT: Jon Hurwitz, Hayden Schlossberg, Josh Heald)

Together again. Billy and I welcome Lisa to *Cobra Kai* Season 3.

With my family at the Season 2 launch of *Cobra Kai*.

Creators, cast, and producers celebrate *Cobra Kai*
at a Paley Center premiere.

a Comic-Con event and we had a good laugh about it. It's interesting to look back years later and reminisce about how it all came to be. One thing has always seemed clear to me with casting, at least when a movie succeeds like *Sixteen Candles* did: The right actor undoubtedly gets the right part.

In the fall of '84, I had what you would call an A-list meeting with a pair of Hollywood heavyweights. I was very excited about the opportunity. *The Karate Kid* was the talk of the town when I sat down with Steven Spielberg and Robert Zemeckis to discuss their new "time traveler" movie. Over the years there have been reports that I turned down this mega-blockbuster franchise, so I figure now may be a good time to tell this particular eighties story from my viewpoint. The three of us met in a New York City hotel suite. It was not a reading audition, meaning I didn't have to perform a scene, even though the script for *Back to the Future* had been sent to me before I sat down with Mr. Zemeckis and Mr. Spielberg. They must have been thinking of me as a potential Marty McFly. The meeting and conversation were fast-paced, upbeat, and positive. I had met Spielberg a few years earlier when he was casting *E.T.: The Extraterrestrial*. Having that experience helped make the conversation more relaxed. I distinctly remember two points that were hit upon during the *Back to the Future* meeting.

One was the importance of an all-American quality to the character, as was written in the script. The concern was that I had a New York accent that would need to be curbed for the character and a distinct East Coast ethnicity. McFly was apple pie, and as I mentioned in chapter 3 of this book, I came up more cannoli. From that point on during the encounter, I did my best to try to cover my New York–ness and be optimistic that I could shed the accent and seem more mainstream mid-America. I didn't have a real read on whether this was effective in the moment, but still, I attempted to enunciate and slow down my speech cadence. I would love to have video playback of what I was doing. I imagine it came off as a hilarious train wreck.

The other exchange I remember from the meeting is when they asked me whether I was bumped by the boy's infatuation with his own mother. Did I feel it was an incestuous problem that audiences would have an issue with? I wish I could say that I had an insightful answer, but I believe I just tap-danced around it and expressed my view that as long as it was entertaining, it should be okay. Not my most brilliant response, but at the time it was met with pleasant nods from the two legendary filmmakers. It's fascinating to me to remember these moments and interactions about something that has become such a famous milestone piece of entertainment. Frankly, it's just so cool to have these eighties stories to tell. Whether I'm talking about getting *The Karate Kid* or not getting *Back to the Future*, people lean in as I elaborate and genuinely love hearing about it. So, with that, I shall continue. . . .

Okay, what did happen after that Zemeckis/Spielberg meeting? At that point, I had received the confirmation that a *Karate Kid* sequel production was to happen in the summer of '85. I was beginning to start my preparation work for *Crossroads* (slated for spring '85) and was studying blues, rock, and classical guitar. I was creatively obsessed with the music and the origin of the blues and its influence on rock and roll. I was excited to make that film and explore those roots. The director was Walter Hill, who had made *The Warriors* and *48 Hrs.*, two very popular films that made an impression on me growing up. I had already heard that the team for *Back to the Future* was unsure whether I was the right fit and would not be making a direct offer. They would, however, be open to having me screen-test for the McFly role along with some other candidates. That test deal would include multiple sequel options, similar to the *Karate Kid* test agreement. Typical Hollywood politics came into play, with one franchise being at Columbia Pictures and the other at Universal Studios, and, in short, the *Back to the Future* discussions didn't go any further.

The wonderful irony to all of this is that the all-American, apple-pie role of Marty McFly was eventually awarded to the perfectly cast, but Canadian, Michael J. Fox. And this was after the role was initially given to Eric Stoltz (a wonderful actor whom I later worked with in the early nineties on a film titled *Naked in New York*). At the end of the day, whether it's Molly Ringwald in *Pretty in Pink*, Matthew Broderick in *Ferris Bueller's Day Off*, Michael J. Fox in *Back to the Future*, or, dare I be this bold, Ralph Macchio in *The Karate Kid*—I said it before and I'll say it again . . . the right actor got the right part.

Now, what is it about eighties movies that makes them so

beloved? And where does *The Karate Kid* sit in the landscape? Well, for one, it seemed to be a simpler time. Or less sensitive. I'm not making a judgment as much as an observation. Everything was way less politically correct. I think that is what audiences find so refreshing about the writing of adult Johnny Lawrence in *Cobra Kai*. The Zabka character is stuck in an eighties mindset with no filter. It becomes entertaining to hear him rattle off what is considered offensive now but was the norm for 1984. Audiences love that element in the writing of the series. He gets away with it because he doesn't know any better and it reads as innocent. When we rewatch the films of that time period, the viewpoints could be interpreted as dated, to say the least. Yet in many cases they were hopeful—not as dark as much of today's programming. Back then, teen angst would often turn to wish fulfillment. Ferris lip-syncing "Twist and Shout" on a parade float down Michigan Avenue. McFly rocking "Johnny B. Goode" on his parents' prom night. Even the stereotypes were embraced. Take *The Breakfast Club*, for example. The jock, the nerd, the princess, etc. *The Karate Kid* had a bit of that as well. The bully, the rich girl, the evil teacher, the wise mentor. It was good-over-evil storytelling. Not too many gray areas, if any. But the audiences loved it and they still do. Despite being dated, many of these movies hold up because of their timeless themes and aspirational qualities.

Perhaps that's why parents share eighties films with their kids seemingly more than films from any other era of movies. They are entertaining and life-affirming. And maybe they provide a bit of escapism from all of the negativity today's generation is subjected to with the world's troubles at their fingertips. It becomes family viewing, tying together yesterday and today. The relatability factor of *The Karate Kid* still feels genuine and current in terms of the bullying and fish-out-of-water scenarios. Despite the eighties of it all, the themes and messaging remain relevant and strong.

As I have stated before, the story resonates across generations on a human level. It might be why *Cobra Kai* is viewed as a "four-quadrant show" in the entertainment industry. It brings together mothers and daughters, fathers and sons. This is something we often hear when the data research is reported from Sony and Netflix. But when it comes to the attraction to the eighties, let's not underplay the impact and influence of the music in those movies too. . . . Ah yes, we all wanted our MTV, and MTV enhanced the box-office performance of the movies!

The eighties were also the birthplace of the music video. The decade when tying film clips into the video for a soundtrack hit became an additional selling tool for both. Who you gonna call? "Ghostbusters." Huey Lewis's "The Power of Love" and Simple Minds' "Don't You (Forget About Me)" were a few heavy hitters in this category. It was Bananarama's "Cruel Summer" for *The Karate Kid* in '84 and "Glory of Love" from Peter Cetera for *Part II* in '86. And who didn't get amped up for Kenny Loggins's "Danger Zone" or mimic the melody of Berlin's "Take My Breath Away" when you think about Cruise and his F-14? Many of these songs are still popular with the next generation. Characters from these films continue to evolve and grow before our eyes in current TV series and movie sequels. I see it in the younger cast on *Cobra Kai*, and with tweens and teens who wear their eighties-rock emblems proudly on their tees—Van Halen, Metallica, AC/DC. It's retro-cool, and that music, like Cobra Kai, seems to never die.

I liked many of those songs, although I didn't fancy either Tears for Fears or Duran Duran, despite the fact that they seemed to own MTV in the eighties. Maybe I had a mullet problem? Then again, I did sport one for a bit myself and was a big hockey fan, so that would probably debunk that theory. For the record, my personal playlist, or should I say the cassette tapes in my car and albums in my room, included U2, Springsteen (of course), the Who, Eric Clapton, Billy Joel, Elvis Costello, Queen, Guns N' Roses, and a fair number of blues records. Add to that some Broadway musical and movie soundtracks, a bit of classical, a random Benny Goodman and His Orchestra record ("Sing, Sing, Sing" royally kicks ass!), and seventies staples like *Frampton Comes Alive!* and Stevie Wonder's *Songs in the Key of Life*. There, that's a snapshot of my varied taste in music at the time. Not too much has changed.

There was also a certain look to eighties films that was unique. Or at least there was a signature feel to many of them. There would always be "the wet-down" on the street anytime we shot a night exterior. A large water truck would spray down the asphalt to give it that glossy black look. Think about it.

The soaking-wet glow of the parking lot at the Twin Pines Mall, where the DeLorean left its flaming track marks in *Back to the Future*. The glistening streets in *Flashdance* and *Beverly Hills Cop*. In virtually every eighties movie, when an exterior night scene takes place, it seems it just stopped raining sixty seconds prior to the action. Walking across the parking lot for the Golf N' Stuff date with Elisabeth Shue, I recall having to navigate through large puddles on the asphalt. But we loved that look. It made everything pop. And when the streetlights and neon signs were reflected in the wet pavement, well, that was the cherry on top!

Another distinctive look of that movie era was fog or atmospheric smoke. Whether it was out in the field or in a suburban kitchen, the air seemed "foggy." The special effects teams would fill the air with a layer of beeswax smoke or use fog sprayers to create the look. Sunlight coming through window blinds would be emphasized by the thickness of the air. The separation of shadows and light would be enhanced by this effect, and it felt distinctly eighties. And I don't believe there was ever a manhole cover that didn't have white smoke billowing out of it against the glistening blacktop. Fog would come from everywhere and at any cost. In *The Karate Kid*, just before Daniel LaRusso gets caught at the fence by the Cobras on Halloween night, if you look closely at the open field, you can locate the source. Daniel passes by a tree in the distance, and you will find the shadowy figure of our special effects guy wafting smoke/fog from his canister. It's as if the base of the tree is smoldering and fog appears in puffy increments. No one caught it or complained. I mean, it was a small price to pay. The atmospheric result was eighties awesome!

Another signature of the decade was the training montage. Well, any montage, for that matter. Montages were king. A simple cinematic concept that reigned as the champ of eighties cinema. Prime examples can be located in *Rocky III* and *Rocky IV*, *Footloose*, *The Breakfast Club*, and *Top Gun*, and arguably the best of all was in *The Karate Kid*. Mini music videos inserted to indicate the passage of time or the growth of a character and/or the plot. In every season of *Cobra Kai* there's a discussion of where the eighties montage will sit in that particular chapter and what totally badass piece of music will underscore it. It's like vintage art revisited and newly framed for today's audience. The eighties music montage was an essential part of the fabric of that era and fits like a glove into our show. It's been an absolute fan favorite every season.

But no matter what the bells or whistles were in that era, *The Karate Kid* and the other films I have referenced stand the test of time mainly due to the heart within their stories. The staying power comes from those moments and images that make an emotional connection with the audience. As with any storytelling, we love these films because we care. We can relate. They strike a chord and harken back to a time that was simpler than today (or at least we may feel that way). That is not to imply that that time was better, per se, but it was simpler. Even with the eighties of it all, the emotional elements seem clear in those movies and firmly grounded in their own reality. I think that's why the films stay in the audience's heart. But man, who doesn't crave some Huey Lewis soundtracking McFly in a skateboard chase, or a Joe Esposito anthem driving LaRusso into the tournament finals!

History repeats itself
Try and you'll succeed
Never doubt that you're the one
And you can have your dreams.
You're the best . . .

Sorry, couldn't resist. Good luck getting *that* out of your head the rest of the day.

CHAPTER SEVEN

Frozen in Time

As I bade farewell to the eighties and entered the nineties, I certainly wasn't as open as I am today to embracing the burden/privilege of being so associated with one famous character. There was for sure a time when I was looking to separate myself from Daniel LaRusso, to avoid being typecast. The climate was changing for me, and I felt a resistance from the entertainment industry to bridging any gap going forward. Prime opportunities were drying up. It felt a little like my time had come and gone. At least it appeared that way from my perspective.

"You don't want him, he's the Karate Kid."

Those were the words from a studio executive when the filmmakers of *My Cousin Vinny* inquired about my potential availability. There was a great deal of pushback to my even securing an audition to play Joe Pesci's Italian American cousin from New York. This was 1991. Interestingly, Ben Stiller and Will Smith were two names on the top of the studio's list as candidates for the college-age students wrongfully accused of murder in Beechum County, Alabama. I, on the other hand, was not, omitted from a list I might have been on just a year prior. But I get it, and I got it even then. I understood how things work. Nevertheless, it was the first real example for me that the wave's crest was now behind me and the rush was over (for the time being). Those names I mentioned were on their way up the mountain as I was sliding down the other side, at least in the minds of the decision makers at that point in time.

As you may imagine, it was frustrating for me, especially in this case, because the role seemed such a perfect fit. I was defiant at first but soon relaxed into the game-playing atmosphere and went in to audition. It was the right thing to do. What seemed a good, if not obvious, casting idea to me played out successfully when I got to prove myself. Thankfully, the filmmakers prevailed over any studio trepidation, and I'm proud to have that one on the résumé. I affectionately call it "the late-for-dinner movie." If *My Cousin Vinny* is on television as you're getting ready . . . you're going to be late for dinner.

I can't pinpoint only one reason for why things slowed for me after the eighties. It was multifactored. Surely, the underwhelming response to *The Karate Kid Part III* was probably part of it. I have often spoken out about the fact that that specific installment of the franchise has never been my favorite. Back then, I felt it didn't grow the character of Daniel LaRusso. There was little evolution. If anything, he went backward, with the story repeating itself. The tone had moved into an even more heightened reality, with some characters bordering on cartoonish. And I still feel that way today. It has never been the film or performance I am most proud of in my career. Though, I must reiterate, having it to use as canon in *Cobra Kai* has only enhanced the writers' ability to dive deeper into ongoing story lines and explore other characters. One prime example is the Terry Silver character, who was part of the overly heightened element in *Part III*. Thomas Ian Griffith is so wonderful with his refined, villainous portrayal of Mr. Silver in *Cobra Kai*. It's one of the highlights for me in the later seasons of the series. Definitely one area that I never thought I would ever revisit. Many of the fans of the "second sequel" are loving the dynamics and how those plot points weave into the current series. It gives us a chance to redeem some of the movie's shortcomings and create engaging conflicts and arcs for the show. Earlier in the book, I mentioned that the creators of *Cobra Kai* have an affinity for certain characters and elements in that film. Without their fandom for *Part III*, *Cobra Kai* might not exist. Who knew? Even in the most unexpected ways, it's always the gift that keeps on giving.

In 1994, there came *The Next Karate Kid*. By then I was in my thirties, and Jerry Weintraub noted to the press that I was too old to continue on in the role. In fact, that is how I learned the film was being made. I saw it in the newspaper. They went with a different writer, a different director, and a different actor for the protagonist. Hilary Swank was Julie Pierce in *The*

Next Karate Kid. Pat Morita reprised the Mr. Miyagi role for that installment as well. To this day, for whatever reason, I have not viewed that movie curtain-to-curtain. I have only seen it in pieces when scrolling through movie channels on television. It was strange for me, as I wasn't in contact with anyone from the franchise during those years. Even Pat Morita and I fell a little out of touch in the early nineties. We rekindled our relationship in the early 2000s, when he met my kids for the first time. This was the point when I presented him with a lifetime achievement award at Lincoln Center in New York City, a story I will elaborate on in a later chapter.

After *My Cousin Vinny*'s release in 1992, I became very focused on my family. My daughter was born that same year and my son three years after that. I was out of the loop with my *Karate Kid* family during that time. Some of this was by design and some was not. That OG family had broken up a bit since neither John Avildsen, Robert Kamen, nor I had anything to do with the Hilary Swank version.

During the nineties, I was attempting to carve another path toward defining my acting career post LaRusso. I participated in some indie films and had guest-star TV roles peppered throughout. However, nothing really broke through. I dove into writing screenplays and some acting on the New York stage during that particular window. I'd had a successful run starring opposite Robert De Niro on Broadway in 1986 in *Cuba and His Teddy Bear*, so I had gained some legit cred in the theater world. With this, I could stay close to my wife and our growing family on the East Coast.

But truth be told, it was challenging coming to grips with Hollywood's labeling and pigeonholing me as the Karate Kid, especially despite my work in *The Outsiders* and the success of *My Cousin Vinny*. Even with the movies in between and a critically acclaimed Broadway run with De Niro, it seemed nothing could alter those pointed views. It was becoming more and more difficult to shake that trademark, especially in the movie and TV world. As years went on and maturity made me a bit wiser, it became silly not to be proud of the legacy. And that's where I sit with it now. But back then I was frustrated to be frozen in time in the eyes of the world and the entertainment industry. It was a challenge for people to see me as anything but the kid who played Daniel LaRusso. And it still is to some extent.

The fact that I look so young for my age only added another element to it all. This may have played a larger part than anything else in the overall perception and branding. I wasn't maturing physically at a "normal" pace, and it created a hurdle in graduating from teenager to young leading-man roles. In later years, I would quip here and there in interviews that I played sixteen for thirty-five years. That always received a good reaction. A little self-deprecating humor went a long way in my shuffling through it all. It's still brought up, even now. "You don't age." I'm not so sure I agree, but I shall take that as a compliment. As long as I can remember, I was always the youngest-looking in the crowd, from junior high school into high school and beyond. I could win a bucketful of stuffed animal toys at any carnival's "Guess Your Age" booth. Those vendors didn't stand a chance. Off by five to seven years no matter what. I call it the Macchio curve: When someone asks how old I was when I played in this movie or that movie, I tell them, "Pick a number, add five-plus years, and you're there." It's not completely accurate and getting less so these days, but it's more humor to counter the perpetual questioning.

I guess if you consider the alternative, one would say I am lucky. "I have good genes," is how I put it most often. I routinely point out that it's my parents' fault that I have been blessed with this curse. And I have learned to playfully handle the ribbing about it over the years. My parents look amazingly young for their age as well. Both my grandmothers had the same blessing. They were very youthful in their appearance as well as how they carried themselves. So, in their honor, I'm going to play this young-looking thing out as long as I can. Even if it further amplifies my being frozen in time in the minds of the masses. At sixty years of age, I am cool with that.

I was a little less cool with it when I visited David Letterman while promoting *My Cousin Vinny*. It led to one of my personal-best defensive zingers on late night. I remember getting the call early in the day that a guest had dropped out and the Letterman show was looking to fill the slot. *Vinny* had just opened, and I was on the short list. I was a big Letterman fan; however, I was a little apprehensive of and intimidated by his quick wit and uncanny sarcasm. I had seen a fair number of celebs just die in the guest chair when they couldn't keep up. So I expressed my concern, though I was flattered that I had been asked. I was assured that he loved *My Cousin Vinny*, so I moved forward with guarded optimism. Plus, this opportunity could give me a chance to reveal another side of myself. After all, I was in a new hit movie; maybe I could alter some of the showbiz industry's preconceived notions, right? I wanted to be loose and focused so as not to screw up my first Letterman spot. And . . . drumroll, please . . .

I had a slight sore throat on that day. It was the beginnings of a cold, and I was feeling a bit under the weather but didn't think it would interfere. The "show must go on" theory. I had been tipped off that the studio would be cold and was advised to bring a jacket and/or scarf for backstage. For comedy you always want the studio cold so the audience stays sharp and doesn't get tired from warm or stuffy surroundings. Comedy = cold. However, Letterman cold is "see your breath" kinda cold. I mean, "rub your hands together for friction warmth before you're introduced" type of cold. And I did, and I was decently sharp. My entrance music was "Glory of Love" from *The Karate*

Kid Part II. Paul Shaffer (Letterman's musical director) went on to inform me that he'd worked on the production of the song when it was being recorded. In essence, he and I had indirectly worked together. That was a nice icebreaker (literally and figuratively), as I was fighting the studio temperature and my worry that things could go even colder in the interview for any number of reasons.

This was 1992, and my daughter had been born a few months prior. Well, this came up while we were on the air, and Letterman could not get over the fact that I was a new dad. Up until that point, the segment had been going smoothly and was as friendly and as easy as anyone would hope for. I was sailing. But then the "age thing" became the subject at hand and it was slightly less than comfortable. I just looked like a kid to him, and he was trying to wrap his head around it. He couldn't understand how it was possible. He began badgering me with rapid-fire questions. They were in good fun, but it was wearing on me and I had to do something. So, I mustered up just enough of my own sarcasm and took a stab at putting a pin in it with this zinger:

"We better hurry up, because I'm due back at the museum in half an hour."

Boom! A roar of hilarity from the crowd, including Paul Shaffer and the band. I cautiously looked to Letterman, thinking he might be positioning himself to come in for the kill. But he just pushed off from his desk with the wheels of his chair gliding him back. He put his hands up in mock surrender. Victory! I think? Maybe? If nothing else, I believe I gained a tiny bit of his respect. The last section of the interview was friendly and complimentary toward me and the newly released Joe Pesci movie I was there to promote. So yes, as one of the "two yoots," I've learned to embrace my youngish appearance and make it fun and entertaining. Even if as a defense mechanism. Now, I am not sure this guest spot on late night ever did anything to help me counter the assumption that I am frozen in time. Nonetheless, I was proud to come out of it with a feather in my Letterman cap.

I led a unique existence as an adult, looking young for my age while being connected to a "kid" who was, and continues to be, *that* iconic, and not just in the United States but the world over. I represent a specific time in people's lives. A window that is often pinpointed as part of the conversation whenever I meet someone for the first time. It's odd but understandable, and certainly unique. Very often people want to discuss where they were when they saw the movie. What they were doing at that time in their lives. How it impacted them.

Think about it: For the most part, the lion's share of people who are introduced to someone for the first time usually have a vast number of possible subjects to discuss. The office party they are attending. Or the restaurant they happen to be dining in. Or the sporting event they're at while they stand in the beer line. They may discuss politics. Perhaps their favorite food or even which school the kids should go to in the fall. But generally, it was different for me. When I met anyone for the first time, the discussion would surround a small window hovering around 1984. The where, what, how, and wow of it all. And when those conversations began, there would often be disbelief that I had kids of my own who were close to LaRusso's age.

This has definitely changed more recently with the success of *Cobra Kai* and the adult Daniel LaRusso. Especially with the younger generation so engaged in the show. But for thirty-five years before *Cobra Kai* took the world by storm, I had to address mostly questions and conversations about a very small window of time. No one cared what I'd had to eat for breakfast or what car I was driving. Or what I had planned for the following week. Or even what might be my next project. It would most often be about *then*. I represented a particular time stamp in people's lives.

I understand it—I played a character who was a part of your childhood. This type of nostalgia is similar to definitive and iconic sports moments that have left lasting impressions on my life. That's how I related to it. Where was I when the US hockey team beat Russia in the 1980 Olympics in Lake Placid? Who was I with when Mookie Wilson chopped the ball down the first-base line and redefined how we remember Bill Buckner in the 1986 World Series? Or what about when a young Joe Montana launched his legacy with a tight spiral to Dwight Clark in the back of the end zone? (My answers: at home with my family; at Shea Stadium with my soon-to-be wife—yes, I was at game six!; and in my friend's den.)

Me, myself, and LaRusso have been frozen in time like goalie Jim Craig, forever wrapped in an American flag, searching for his dad in the stands after the Miracle on Ice. These former athletes must have at least the same lower-back pain I have when I get out of bed in the morning. But we don't want to think about *the* Joe Montana that way, or even imagine it. We don't want to see him squinting at a dinner menu. We don't want to hear about his creaking knees or the pain in his joints or whether he has to pee more than once in the middle of the night. (Sorry, folks, but it happens.) We just want to see Montana throwing the game-winning touchdown in Super Bowl XXIII.

I recently learned that Jim Craig is an accomplished motivational speaker. Maybe he has receding gray hair, but all I can say is that if we ever run into him, he had better be wrapped in red, white, and blue! Right? Well, that's how people would look at me. If I'm out with my wife and kids, people affectionately tell me I make them feel old. But still, I'm a warm and wonderful time stamp in their lives. So, I became at peace with my specialness during all of those years, understanding what it meant to people and that they weren't intentionally pinning me to only one sliver of time. I found a positive spin. I'd use those encounters as inspiration when I heard their personal stories of what *The Karate Kid* had meant to them, or even what I meant to them, for that matter. That's how I chose to accept and benefit from this alter ego and blurred-lined existence. Later in the book I will showcase a few examples of this.

Still, even with that, years later, a jarring moment came when I got wind that a remake was in the works. A new version of *The Karate Kid* outside of the Miyagiverse without me, Pat, or our characters or any ties to them. Seriously? No way. Too soon, right? It was like 2008. I smile at the irony of my initial reaction. I find this such an amusing observation as I look at it now. I spent twenty years trying to prove I'm not a kid anymore, and then when I heard they were remaking my biggest movie, all of a sudden, I was like, *Hey, why are they rushing everything!* I was at the Sundance Film Festival at the time. My short film *Love Thy Brother* had premiered there a few years earlier, so I was back as a filmmaker, networking at the festival while also promoting an indie film I had in the lineup. I was making my way up the Main Street strip one afternoon when a *TMZ*-like reporter stopped me and asked, "So what do you think about Will Smith remaking *The Karate Kid* for his son, Jaden?"

I recall being caught off guard trying to process the concept. I remember saying that I am not the biggest fan of most remakes. I personally don't enjoy movies as much when I know how they're going to end. I then went on to say that I was hoping there would be more original content coming out of Hollywood soon. But I wished everyone good luck and success and thought it was cool to know the story still had great relevance. Well, as often is the case when something is spun for clickbait, the headline the next day read:

MACCHIO SLAMS REMAKE

And within forty-eight hours of that, there came a call from Will Smith himself. I was tipped off by one of my reps that he was going to reach out. I assumed he had seen or heard of the headline. I was curious and wasn't sure what to expect, so there was heightened anticipation. He led off the call with a playful "Look, I know I'm messin' with your baby . . . but I promise I will do it right . . . respect, homage, respect." He was cool and the intentions were clear. I reminded him that we'd met at the *My Cousin Vinny* audition and that it was one of the rare occasions where I had gotten the part and he hadn't. I alluded to his megastar movie successes that had followed almost immediately after that audition day. He chuckled. We had an upbeat conversation with a lot of laughs and mutual respect exchanged. I cleared up any concern that I was angry, explaining the sensationalized tabloidlike headline. And in return, he offered to involve me in the remake in any way I wanted and said that the door was open. I felt very strongly that stepping back and allowing him and his team to reimagine the story their own way would be best for all. I had no real reason to get involved, even on the periphery. I didn't even know what the script was. I had no idea of the tone they were going for. All I knew was that Jaden was substantially younger than the Daniel LaRusso character I had played.

It became clear as we were winding down the conversation that there was an additional reason for the call. Will wanted Jaden to say hello to me and vice versa. He asked me if it would be okay to put him on the phone, and of course I said yes, absolutely. It was a brief exchange. Jaden said he was honored to speak to me, and I told him to be good to his character. To kick some butt and have fun doing it. But I couldn't avoid the awareness that, in the moment, I felt very much like an Obi-Wan to a young Skywalker. As if I were handing off the lightsaber to a new-generation Jedi warrior. Now, to that point, that sentiment is actually far more relevant today in terms of the young cast I work with on *Cobra Kai*. It resonates on a much higher level with me and those wonderful actors in our series. *Cobra Kai* is part of the Miyagiverse, whereas the Jaden Smith remake is not. But at that moment in time, on the call with Jaden and Will, that's the way it felt to me. I would now be referenced as "the original" Karate Kid. As if I didn't own it solely anymore. And internally, on the day, that probably felt slightly more bitter than sweet.

There were wishes for good luck exchanged as we finished the conversation and sent well-wishes to all. The truth is I was pleased to have gotten that call. I was glad Will had reached out and happy we had spoken. As it turned out, the 2010 remake had pretty much the same story as the original, but it felt extremely different as a movie. Columbia Pictures invited me to the big Los Angeles premiere, and I took in the new version with an industry audience. It felt so very far removed from our *Karate Kid* franchise. But it made sense to be there. Billy and some of the other OG Cobras attended as well. It was also good to reunite with Weintraub that night. It would be the last time I saw Jerry. He told me on a few occasions over the evening that he loved me and how I was such a big part of his life. But as was often the case with Jerry around his industry peers, in his vintage Brooklyn accent, he would introduce me as "the kid that bought me a couple of houses." We'd knowingly smile at each other with a friendly head shake, acknowledging that Jerry was being Jerry. I told him that night that I believed the remake would only enhance the legacy of the original. And as time has gone on, I can say with confidence that I was right. That film did well at the box office; however, the staying power of the original franchise was never usurped. *Cobra Kai* alone may be proof of that.

On a semi-selfish note, going to the premiere of the remake was also a chance for me to talk about *Wax On, Fuck Off,* a video that I had made with the team at FunnyorDie.com. I partnered with a veteran TV director, my friend Todd Holland, to craft this mock trailer for a fictitious documentary on the current state of my career. It ran a tight four minutes and, in my opinion, was perfectly executed. This was sandwiched a few years between the release of the "Sweep the Leg" music video for Billy and my guest appearance on *How I Met Your*

Mother. It launched the day before the remake opened and instantly went viral. Yes, timing is everything. The piece was kind of my answer to myself about not sitting idly by and doing nothing as the 2010 version hit the screens. I had to keep busy, and this was my satirical pet project at the time. It was a chance to meet the frozen-in-timers head-on, being that it was co-created by me, on my terms. But most important, the thing was damn funny! And still is, though somewhat dated, thanks to the recent surge and success.

The concept was simple: a reverse intervention. This was during a time when bad behavior seemed to be rewarded, if not celebrated, in Hollywood. So, I came up with an idea to play on that concept and I ran with it. I poked fun at the young-looking Macchio, who is so overly nice and wholesome that even his family and friends can't take it anymore, launching Ralph into a self-inflicted makeover in an attempt to become cool and relevant again in Hollywood. It really is quite entertaining. The more badass he attempts to become (cocaine, hookers, alcohol), the more deeply he fails. It's a never-coming-of-age, comedically tragic cautionary tale. We had some amazing actors and friends come in to cameo and join in on the joke party (including Tiffany Haddish, Kevin Connolly, and Molly Ringwald, to name a few). The end result, in my humble opinion, is what I called "the best four minutes you will have all day." The critics really respected it, and it was so well received by the fans too. At the remake's premiere, this led to a lot of red-carpet attention about the video, and therefore it took some of the edge off the question "How does it feel to have another *Karate Kid* out there?" It was a cathartic elixir for me as I went through that chapter. Whether it be on Letterman or before a premiere, a little self-deprecating creative humor is a go-to that often works for me. And so, I went for it. If you can spare a few minutes or have the desire, have a laugh on me, as I believe *Wax On, Fuck Off* can still be found online. Enjoy!

As I circle my attention back to the present day, I would have to say for sure the frozen-in-time-ness has waned a significant amount. The popularity of *Cobra Kai* has made everything about the *Karate Kid* universe current and present in entertainment. We now know a version of Daniel LaRusso as a middle-aged man. The audience visits a world where LaRusso exists who isn't thirty-plus years old.

Still, the teen version of Daniel LaRusso is unmatched in regard to worldwide, generational recognition. He's had a head start. Nothing really can compare with the iconic role that Daniel-san represents in American movie history. For the most part, the fans are still saying, "Hey, aren't you the Karate Kid?" However, the Netflix effect has had a powerful, global impact. With that, the balance has shifted ever so slightly, with kids occasionally coming to me with "Hey, aren't you the guy who plays Daniel LaRusso on *Cobra Kai*?" And I must admit, it is bittersweet and refreshing all at the same time. It's proof of the fact that the legacy is evolving and continuing to grow. LaRusso is reaching an even wider audience, if we can believe that.

But to certain fans out there, he and I still remain a blast from yesteryear. It's difficult to separate me and LaRusso, as we remain frozen to more than a handful, born into a certain time frame in their minds. As I've said, I am thoroughly at peace with this and cheer their fandom and respect for the character. But I do have days when I might playfully retort with some good-natured sarcasm of my own: "No, I'm not from New Jersey, and Pat Morita didn't really work in my apartment building. But thank you for asking. Oh, and one more thing . . .

"The kick was legal!"

CHAPTER EIGHT

Theories and Debates
(and the Birth of *Cobra Kai*)

Was the crane kick truly illegal? Who is actually the real bully? Was Neil Patrick Harris's *How I Met Your Mother* character correct? Was William Zabka's Johnny given a raw deal? Was Daniel really the "bad guy"? *Cobra Kai* meets all of this head-on and deals with it in the cleverest way. It spotlights these theories and debates with altered viewpoints depending on who is telling the story and from what angle it is being told. But before that, with the arrival of the internet, social media, and the explosion of fan conventions, these debates and theories had raged on for decades. . . .

And they *still* do. . . .

For me, I think the first time that I heard the "real Karate Kid" theory was in 2009. It might have been out there before then, but this was my first glimpse. It apparently was born in the writers' room of *How I Met Your Mother* during their fourth season. I recall one or both of my kids calling me into our den to see an episode entitled "The Stinsons." This episode is when Barney Stinson first expresses his personal allegiance to the only character to ever root for in *The Karate Kid* in his opinion—his hero, Johnny Lawrence of the Cobra Kai dojo. It was so perfectly fitting that the Barney character, the guy who often possessed an undercutting and self-centered personality, would root for the bully in his favorite childhood movie. At first, I rolled my eyes at the idiotic concept, but I quickly realized it was kind of brilliant. All the other characters in the sitcom's scene were baffled by this theory, as they all saw Daniel LaRusso as the film's hero—that was general knowledge and the obvious line of thinking. They felt that way, and of course I felt that way too. However, the choice to align Barney's take-no-prisoners approach to life with an affinity for Johnny Lawrence opened up a new perspective on and interpretation of the film. It turned the conventional wisdom on its head. Add the flawless delivery of Neil Patrick Harris, and it was perfect entertainment.

I watched that episode a few times over, sharing it and laughing with my kids. It was fun for them to see their dad's movie referenced in one of their favorite TV shows. The experience of watching a callback to the original film with my kids had happened a few times previously in other series and movies too. It was always enjoyable to see a nod to the film's place in popular culture and the world of entertainment. But here, there was a perspective twist that made this feel really different. And so, I was wrestling with the sting and the brilliance of it simultaneously.

I then began to defend LaRusso in my head. Sort of playing over scenes in my mind's eye that would clearly debunk this Barney Stinson theory. For nearly a quarter of a century, I had walked the streets having portrayed the true hero of a classic coming-of-age movie. And now there was a new and very smart angle from a different perspective. The saving grace in my mind was that it was singularly affiliated with Barney's self-absorbed character. Any levelheaded audience member would get the comedy, the ridiculousness. We could all understand the absurdity of this point of view. But was there a sliver of truth there? That LaRusso stole Johnny's girl at the point when he was going to try to win her back? That Johnny, as defending All Valley champ, an excellent martial artist, lost to an illegal kick to the face? That LaRusso barely even knew karate? That he couldn't leave well enough alone and provoked all of those beatdowns by the Cobra Kai? . . .

. . . Nah!

I concluded that this was a one-off Barney-centric theory. But brilliant it was, and bravo to the execution of it through that show's character. Now, I don't recall exactly how long it was after that theory initially seeped into the consciousness of the TV and internet world, but I do vividly remember what the setting was for my next gut-punch from the left side of fandom. I was participating in a fan convention and was at a table meeting fans and taking pictures. It was the usual crowd of folks with eight-by-tens, books, and memorabilia from *The Karate Kid*, *The Outsiders*, *Crossroads*, and *My Cousin Vinny*.

Some come dressed as characters to show off their pretty fanatic loyalty. In this one particular instance, there was a fan dressed in a shower costume for the cosplay competition that would happen later in the evening. The attention to detail was impeccable. The entire getup was intact, including the San Diego Chargers jersey LaRusso wore under the polka-dot shower curtain. Silver tinsel extended down from the showerhead to simulate running water. The guy looked as if he were going to the Halloween dance in the movie. The only blemish that kept it from perfect accuracy was that he was wearing the *hachimaki* headband—LaRusso was not wearing that in the scene. However, it made for a very impactful, all-encompassing presentation. We took some pictures and I applauded his exquisite costume work after I learned he had constructed it all by hand himself. They obviously call them "fan conventions" for a reason. And then, from behind the shower curtain, an image. Literally from behind the curtain, I for the first time saw another fan's T-shirt. One that I had not seen before. It was a picture of the Johnny Lawrence character standing in his Cobra Kai *gi* with a hashtag that read: "#Justice4Johnny." *Wait, what?*

This particular guy approached me with a cat-that-ate-the-canary smirk as he was looking to get my autograph on a *Karate Kid* poster. I referenced his T-shirt and he went on to say, "Hey, man, you took his girl and scored on an illegal kick to the face." A bunch of LaRusso loyalists in the crowd started yelling, "Bullshit, Daniel's our hero," "Don't listen to this guy,

Ralph," "Miyagi-Do forever!" I think I had a big smile on my face, as this was beyond entertaining to me. To witness the people coming together in defense of their belief in good over evil. Then, within a few seconds of that support . . . farther back in the line, from a distance, there began a chant from a couple of guys in skeleton costumes. In a singsong fashion, they repeated, "Co-bra Kai, Co-bra Kai, Co-bra Kai." And there it was. It was in that moment that it became clear to me that this was no Barney Stinson one-off. A friendly shouting match ensued. And it was *game on*!

These experiences segued into Comic-Con panels that I would do on occasion with Billy and sometimes Martin Kove as well. I was outnumbered onstage two-to-one, but the chanting and fan allegiances would vary and be split. Team LaRusso would defend their childhood hero and proclaim they'd be loyal to Miyagi-Do for life, while Team Lawrence would swear that he was the victim, seeking revenge. As for John Kreese, most everyone saw him as the true villain, though Marty would claim his character was "misunderstood." It was fascinating to watch all of the devotion coming from these fans. The fan base cares so much for these characters and will campaign so hard for their beliefs. They took it all to heart, and it was conclusive evidence that this film had had such a profound impact on their lives. The admiration for it seemed to be growing in intensity. I believed it was due to the internet's ability to connect people from around the world. That, coupled with these conventions, which were an outlet for pop-culture enthusiasts to come together and celebrate their favorites and share their opinions and feelings. One thing was undeniable, a constant no matter what side of the debate they were on. *The Karate Kid* inspired passion. And at that time, more than ten years into the new millennium, it was building, not waning.

In August 2015, a video titled *The Karate Kid: Daniel Is the REAL Bully* went viral on YouTube. It is a clever, truth-twisting, highly entertaining documentary-like breakdown of the events of the original movie. The voice-over leads off with "*The Karate Kid* is the story of Daniel, a violent sociopath who moves to a California town and begins tormenting a local boy and his friends." The video has millions of views and was picked up by many online magazine outlets. I will expose some of its flawed theories shortly in this chapter, but this video was a turning point in reaching a lot of people. Many would ask me if I had seen it and what I thought. It is actually extremely well done and only added to the buildup and thirst of the fans for more of these characters in their lives. In 1984, no one was not rooting for Daniel LaRusso. But for a long time since, a lot of people had been rooting for more story ideas from the *Karate Kid* universe. And man, did I hear a lot of them. Thankfully, I waited for the right time.

I can't begin to share all of the pitches and ideas I had heard over thirty years on how and why I should return to the

LaRusso well. But I do have some of the keepers that are well worth presenting. Especially at this juncture, when I look smart for waiting and only agreeing to *Cobra Kai*. Phew! I don't blame many of the fans, writers, and producers who would share with me their reasoning or ideas for a reboot or sequel concept. I understood that for the most part, it all still stemmed from the love of the original film. But this was a big part of my legacy. I was extremely protective and held this role and that movie to such a high personal standard that it would be difficult for anyone to break through that. Now, in the early days—say, the late 1990s, when I first started hearing ideas—I was pretty much at a point where I wasn't willing to listen. If you recall, this was when I was actively trying to separate from the typecasting. However, as time went on, I would slowly open one ear at a time and attempt to be flexible enough to at least hear them out. I must admit on most occasions it was challenging to get past the first few sentences.

- *Miyagi dies tragically and comes back as a ghost to guide you.*

- *You have a kid who is a bully and you need to be the Miyagi to your troubled kid . . . who also has a drug problem.*

- *Ali is pregnant with Johnny's child and you can't deal even though you're now married to Kumiko.*

Those are just a few that stick in my mind. The best part is that they were completely serious and came from a perspective of trying to help. It was less about "I have a great idea" and more about "I want to get you back." Upon recollection, that still brings me joy. I mean, I do have the greatest, most caring fans. But at the time, I could only smile through the pain of some of these story concepts.

Then there was one of my favorites. It was delivered by a screenwriter to both John Avildsen and myself at a lunch with two studio executives. This was all and everything that is both great and terrible about Hollywood. I believe we were having the lunch to discuss a separate movie project that never did come to fruition. This was after the Hilary Swank version, *The Next Karate Kid,* had come and gone. I remember the enthusiasm with which the writer gave his elevator pitch to John, me, and the studio execs. If you recall, John had directed both *Rocky* and *The Karate Kid,* so that lent itself to this writer's conceptual idea. It was basically a version of this:

"What if Rocky Balboa had a kid and Daniel-san had a kid and they were both fuckups and you, Ralph and Stallone, come together between New Jersey and Philadelphia to join in a Miyagi/Mickey style of fight training. People would go nuts!"

A pregnant pause. It seemed to last for ten minutes, though it was probably only four seconds. Suspended animation. How to process it and respond? The most vivid image in my mind is the lean-in by the two studio executives, as if they were attempting to will it to make sense. John and I shared a mystified look about the concept of this crossover idea. My mind raced to gather visions of Stallone and me running through the slums of Newark. Then John burst into laughter, simply responding that it would not work and was a forced idea. I believe he diplomatically said he wasn't interested in combining those two franchises or those characters. Clearly this was before DC Comics and Marvel changed the landscape of the cinematic superhero world. What did we know? But for that moment it was both intriguing and hilarious. The executives also agreed it wouldn't work; however, they could not mask their disappointment that a big idea had fallen through. Like a prize fish was being reeled in and just when it got to the side of the boat, the line snapped. It was a classic Hollywood show-business moment I'll never forget.

There were a fair number of other nudges and "Come on, man!"'s over the years, from one-line blurbs to more realized versions of how and why to revisit Daniel LaRusso. But it was all too precious to me to risk any one of the "years later" concepts that could spoil the legacy of the original. For the most part they were shortsighted ideas. And I wasn't inspired (at the time) to dance a solo, without the ability to incorporate the Miyagi character. That partnership was paramount. It was easier to just say no thank you.

And I was at peace with that. I remember being asked, "Where do you think LaRusso is now? What happened to him?" This was probably around 2010, when the remake was out. And I didn't really have a perfect answer. I never dove into or considered the "What ever happened to . . . ?" question. Whatever happened to Daniel was whatever you saw on-screen. That's where it ended. But as I tapped into it, my first instinct was that Daniel and Miyagi would have returned to Okinawa, the setting for *The Karate Kid Part II*. Both characters had love story lines that had never been resolved or even brought up again. Those stories had been abandoned. I think in real life, that is where LaRusso would have returned to. At the least to further explore that romantic relationship with Kumiko. But that never materialized, nor was it in the screenwriting cards. The studio chose a different direction. I also didn't really have the action story mapped out to make it exciting and worthy of a fully realized film. For the longest time, everything always fell short of the original film and the pedestal I kept it on. So, again, my theory, at the time, was that it was easier to let it exist only as it was. It had become a classic. Let it be.

As I indicated earlier, Billy was always more open to exploring than I was. He and I would discuss it from time to time, and after a while I did start to loosen my grip on my self-imposed mandate, allowing a little light to shine in on a seed of an idea for our two characters and how and where something might or could bring them together. We even got to the early stages of development on a short-form concept featuring our characters for the internet or a cable comedy channel, but it never panned out—thankfully. Something bigger and better was on its way.

I had just come off my appearance on Comedy Central's roast of Rob Lowe, my castmate from *The Outsiders*, when I received a call from one of my reps. The *Harold and Kumar* writers and their friend, the creator of *Hot Tub Time Machine*, wanted to reach out to me on a TV series idea they were working on. It involved characters from *The Karate Kid*. A few more calls with my manager and lawyer took place to gain a better understanding of what this was. *But wait a minute, the guys who write rated-R stoner comedies want to create something born from the* Karate Kid *universe? Well, okay.* There was just something about the timing of all of this that struck me. The recent shift in my willingness to listen led me to move forward with baby steps. A meeting was set in New York City to hear them out. This was in late September 2016.

Jon, Josh, and Hayden flew in from Los Angeles and delivered to me a very well-thought-out pitch for *Cobra Kai* during a three-hour lunch at the Greenwich Hotel. It was a ton of information to download, and my head was spinning as I tried to grasp it all in one sitting. They led off with the word *bullying*. They tied that theme into their love of the *Karate Kid* franchise and how they wanted to make a continuation story. Not a reboot or redo. They had such a clear, passionate vision and respect for the franchise that I couldn't help but take them seriously, despite the fact that, at first, I had an internal gasp upon hearing the series title, *Cobra Kai*, and processing the Johnny Lawrence redemption factor in it all. But I did believe they held the fans' interest at heart, since they themselves were the fans. That was undeniable based on their knowledge of the movies and the attention to character details. These fellas knew way more than I did about *The Karate Kid*. Every nook and cranny of the landscape. They were well-versed superfans, and I appreciated that.

The element of their pitch that gained the most traction with me (besides their understanding that Mr. Miyagi would need to have a strong presence in the series in order for me to consider it) was the discussion of the teen characters Miguel, Samantha, and Robby. Hearing the story areas for the next-generation characters made me feel there was room for longevity and rich cross-generational storytelling that didn't solely rely on the two older guys who couldn't get past their high school rivalry. There was a lot of forward thinking on their part, and that was impressive. They carefully listened to my thoughts and concerns, and we spoke of how protective I was of the character. It was a very effective if not mind-bending first meeting. With my wheels turning, I walked uptown on Greenwich Street toward Penn Station. I rode back home on a Long Island Rail Road train, mirroring the ride after my first meeting with Avildsen all those years ago. There were one or two more long phone calls in the days that followed before I eventually signed on to join the party, but that's how it began to unfold.

I learned in that Greenwich Hotel meeting that before they met with me, everyone associated on the business side of the franchise was on board, including Billy. They came to me last. At least that's how it felt. The fact that they were pitching the guy who played Daniel LaRusso a show called *Cobra Kai*, coupled with the fact that they were mainly associated with stoner comedies, might have added height to their last hurdle. I think they might have been tipped off that I had reservations about returning to the role. Having all in order before we met proved to be a wise move.

After digesting things overnight, I called Billy the day after the meeting. He answered on the first ring with "I was waiting for this call." I could sense that smirk coming right through the phone. It was a good conversation. We expressed to each other our excitement as well as our reservations. We shared our views and perspectives. Billy had worked with Josh Heald on *Hot Tub Time Machine*, so he already had a connection with him. I believe Jon and Hayden had visited the set when Billy was working, so he had met them as well. I was definitely the last guy in there, but I certainly knew how important a piece I'd be to the puzzle.

For me it was always about protecting the legacy of Daniel LaRusso and the film franchise. Making sure the integrity was upheld and homage was always paid to the *Karate Kid* created back on the set in 1983. And I believe for Billy it was the same. The difference here is he was being pitched the Johnny Lawrence redemption story and I was being pitched how Daniel LaRusso fit into that world. I needed to find "balance" in it to inspire me to sign on. Jon, Josh, and Hayden were very much aware of that from the start, and I was not shy about expressing it. They listened and reassured me about it all, and I made the decision. It still took a leap of faith even though I trusted my gut feeling that this was the right team. I jumped in not fully knowing the temperature of the water, but I knew it was the perfect time for a swim. The deals were hashed out and we began to set up the network pitches for:

Cobra Kai: The Karate Kid Saga Continues . . .

The networks/streamers that were targeted were Amazon, Netflix, TBS, Hulu, YouTube, and HBO. It was one heck of a week. In the various conference rooms, with top creative executives in attendance, the three writers had everything organized and well crafted. They took turns explaining all and everything the show could be. Billy and I had our interjections and characters peppered into the presentation. We even had a sizzle reel with clips from *The Karate Kid* and other visuals on where the story would go, picking it up thirty-four years after the events of the under-eighteen All Valley Karate Championship. It was an absolute home run. We had multiple offers right away. From the start, Netflix was where we always wanted to land. But YouTube won the first round, and consequently the first two seasons would stream on their premium platform. It took a minute, but eventually we landed where we wanted to be, the biggest streaming service on the planet—Netflix.

The "fan" reactions to Billy and I in the same room together, even from the biggest, most seasoned Hollywood executives, was fascinating. It speaks to the depth and impact of our characters and *The Karate Kid*'s place in society. More than a few times during our pitch meetings, we were able to see the eager excitement in their eyes. The smiles on their faces. Their palpable uneasiness, as if they could not understand how we could be on the same side of the table having fun and not trying to beat the crap out of each other. It's amazing how geek-out fandom shows itself in all types and at all levels. I mean, we're actors, folks! We don't hate each other. It was so much fun to have that type of reaction in the room when so often those meetings are stiff and formal. What a blast we had, and what a victory it was. However, we still had to go out and make a show that would hit the target and deliver on the promise. Fortunately for Billy and me, Jon, Josh, and Hayden had a laser-focused vision and delivered it perfectly.

There was a pinpoint moment when Billy and I knew we really had something with *Cobra Kai*, even before the show ever aired or we'd even seen one frame of it. It was on set. Our first scene together as adult Johnny and Daniel. The first time we stepped in front of the camera and back into the skins of these characters after thirty-four years. It was instantaneous from the first rehearsal, before the cameras ever rolled. Deeper and more organic than I had ever expected. We had this synergetic chemistry. A knowing and understanding of the miles and years between us. It was like not a minute had passed in thirty-plus years, save for a few wrinkles and receding hairlines.

The teen spirit was intact, yet life had been lived. Wisdom had been gained. But the boys would be boys. There was rich character history and we tapped into it instinctively.

The scene was in episode 102. LaRusso visits Lawrence in his newly resurrected Cobra Kai dojo when he hears that Johnny beat up a couple of teenagers. They have a tense exchange that includes undercutting insults and posturing. A standoff that is framed in virtually a mirror image of where they stood on the mat at the All Valley final decades prior. It seemed effortless for both Billy and me to bring forth the nuances and colors that played under the dialogue. After the first take, we had this silent conversation as we gazed at each other from across the mat, both recognizing the "wow" in it all. Words truly cannot express how that moment felt. I didn't recall ever feeling that way working with him back in 1983. Perhaps, as I alluded to earlier, it was because for the most part, anytime we were together back then, it involved yelling or ass-kicking. But as men, with historical cinematic lives lived, there were subtleties and layers that came to the surface. A connection to a film and story that we'd shared as we'd walked in our respective shoes over the past thirty-four years. That right there was the secret sauce that made it so delicious. And then we knew . . . we had something.

So much care goes into the making of the show. Jon, Josh, and Hayden set that tone. It is love for the film that inspired the creation of *Cobra Kai*. They wanted to explore what happened to the "bully" and how one was impacted by the "hero"—and where those lines could be blurred while diving into the nuances of these two adult characters. Then they brilliantly built out the world and next-generation cast off of Daniel and Johnny.

And voilà! Here we are. Rocking it all on Netflix as the saga continues into its fifth season. The show shines a bright light on the theories and debates about *The Karate Kid.* That's a large part of its driving narrative and success: taking it all to a higher level with many of the characters. Whether it be through Mary Mouser's Samantha LaRusso (Daniel's daughter) and her rivalry with Tory (Peyton List's character), or Xolo Maridueña's Miguel and his battles with Robby (Johnny's son), portrayed by Tanner Buchanan. Both of whom have dated Samantha. Not to mention the showdown between Courtney Henggeler's Amanda LaRusso (Daniel's wife) and the sinister Sensei John Kreese. Yes, *Cobra Kai is* a karate soap opera. And it achieves that status in the best possible way, somehow always grounding itself with goose bumps and heartstrings as the characters navigate their tangled webs. The tone at times is different, but a common ground it shares with the movie is in its *heart.* And without that, it would not work.

Flashing forward to today, the beauty in all of this is how *Cobra Kai,* being a long-form narrative series, allows us to explore all different types of landscapes and areas in the *Karate Kid* universe, even if it's in an unlikely direction, one that

I would not have expected. *Cobra Kai*'s Daniel LaRusso may have landed in a different place than where I might have believed *The Karate Kid*'s Daniel LaRusso would have landed. However, the series allows multiple story lines and concepts to play out, and we are able to visit many of the areas of the original franchise. This is due to the brain trust of the creators. It has been rich and entertaining no matter where you sit with your views on the theories and debates.

Where do I myself sit with the "real Karate Kid" theory? I have had many opportunities to give my thoughts on this. In a nutshell, a kid who might possess a little feistiness and a tendency not to back down does not make a villain. Or a bully, for that matter. Those personality traits do not warrant the punishment of five-on-one beatdowns and constant berating from a teen karate gang. The heart of *The Karate Kid* lies in Mr. Miyagi and Daniel. Truth be told, the movie *is* Miyagi. And therefore, his student *is* the real Karate Kid. I believe even the naysayers would not argue with that. But it's so much damn fun to point a finger at the imperfections and blemishes, as was done in the *Daniel Is the REAL Bully* fan video. An editorial he said/he said. Super clever, but you can poke holes in its twisted theory. I say if they ever do a sequel to that video, it should focus on the Freddy Fernandez character. He's the kid who invited LaRusso to the beach party at the start of the story. Then he abandoned Daniel with his bloodied face in the sand after he suffered the first beating from Johnny Lawrence. It's Freddy's fault! Freddy deserves the blame. Then again, without Freddy's invite, we have no story. We can go on and on. And they do, and that's just so amazing. That we care enough to defend our viewpoints.

Now . . . was the kick illegal? When we made the film, that was never a discussion. Miyagi also stole a black belt for Daniel to wear so he could compete. Was that legal? I think not. But we did need a climax, people. It's a movie! There was more emphasis on Cobra Kai semifinalist Bobby's illegal strike to the knee that sent LaRusso to the locker room injured and Mr. Miyagi rubbing his hands together for the magical Okinawan fix, leading to the official "Daniel LaRusso's gonna fight!" I have argued that Johnny's blatant elbow to LaRusso's already injured knee in the final match is conclusively illegal. But boy, did it make for high stakes and good movie drama. I joked with Jimmy Fallon on *The Tonight Show*—when we did a sketch game entitled "The Final Word," where I defended LaRusso as previously injured (illegally) and on one leg—that in the climactic moment, Daniel LaRusso was being charged and attacked by Johnny Lawrence and instinctively jumped to defend himself, therefore Johnny literally ran into the kick. The Karate Kid was forced to defend himself. Remember, *karate for defense only*. I concluded that a defensive move against an imminent attack could not be illegal, and I rested my case. I, as always, stand with LaRusso!

I am smiling as I type this. I mean, it's so silly and so mind-blowing. We made this little coming-of-age martial arts movie. And sure, Johnny was a victim of a bad teacher. And he was going to try to "make it right" with Ali before LaRusso came to town. And even though he tortured LaRusso and beat the crap out of him repeatedly, Daniel did douse him with water as he was innocently rolling a joint. But can you blame him?

Currently, *Cobra Kai* has somewhat altered the emphasis of the original film's fan theories and debates. It now has the ongoing narrative of Daniel and Johnny as adults guiding it. Their present-day story is unfolding with each season of the show. However, whenever I was asked at a panel discussion if it bothers me that anyone would question Daniel LaRusso's heroics in *The Karate Kid*, I always had this straightforward response: "When you make a movie that twenty or thirty years later people still obsess and debate about, therefore continuing to keep it relevant and important . . . it's *awesome!*"

My humble admission of how I viewed it all would prompt applause and cheers. And then I would wait for the applause to fade and find just the right moment to button it with . . .

"But Johnny was still a dick!" And I'd seal it with a wink.

CHAPTER NINE

Impact and Inspiration

In early 2021, I participated in two virtual visits with military service members from around the world. These USO events were coordinated by Sony Pictures Television, which produces *Cobra Kai* for Netflix. For the initial one, I was partnered with Yuji Okumoto (who portrays Chozen Toguchi), along with Jon, Josh, and Hayden, and we connected with American troops in Okinawa, Japan. Kadena Air Base is located in Okinawa, the setting for *The Karate Kid Part II* and part of a highlighted story line in *Cobra Kai* season 3. For the second USO experience, I was joined by Billy and the three guys to speak virtually to troops from military base locations in Indiana; Kansas; and Anchorage, Alaska. That one was streamed worldwide by the USO. The theme of these virtual meet-and-greet celebrations was the character transition from classic movie franchise to current television series. We would hear personal and powerful stories with parallels drawn from the *Karate Kid* universe.

During one of the Zoom sessions, a serviceman in his forties became emotional when speaking of his dad and their collective service in the military. He locked his eyes on whatever camera device he was communicating through to make sure his message was received. His voice cracked as he talked about the importance of *The Karate Kid* in his life and referred to me personally as his *hero*. I made sure I leaned in to assure him that I was focused on what he was saying. We were both doing our best to have an "in person" moment through today's technology during the COVID-19 pandemic. But while the setting was new, the sentiment wasn't. I have experienced countless exchanges like this one over the years, with people from all walks of life. I always receive these sentiments modestly and as an innocent misdirect, since Daniel LaRusso is the cinematic hero and I only wear the skin of that character as an actor. I certainly choose to carry the LaRusso torch with pride, respect, and humility. Perhaps that is the reason for the blurred line between actor and character in these cases, why someone might assume I'm a hero or, maybe more on point, a role model. Regardless, it's overwhelming to grasp what a pillar of strength Daniel LaRusso and his cinematic story have become over the years. In this case, when faced with the unimaginable challenges of his service, this man was somehow inspired by me, when in turn, and in truth, I am inspired by him. My point being, the impact and inspiration of this film and character are so gratifying. Perhaps more for me than for anyone else.

Bullying/Mentorship/Wish Fulfillment

These underlying themes from *The Karate Kid* have been at the core of innumerable experiences I have had with people who drew strength and inspiration from Daniel LaRusso and the way his journey through adolescence mirrored and connected with their own on multiple levels. As I approach forty years of this character's existence, the number of occasions when I have crossed paths with someone who longed for a Mr. Miyagi in their life at one time or another seems infinite. Or maybe they drew a comparison between their own lives and an experience in the film's story, or they felt alone or like an outsider and this film and character connected to them emotionally, maybe providing a spark of empowerment in overcoming their own obstacles. Personal stories like these have been shared with me by fans or passersby from every corner of the world.

I was in an airport more than a few years back when a woman approached me with her son. He was probably at most fourteen years old. I believe his name was Brian. He was a slight kid, fairly quiet, and at first Mom did most of the talking. She shared with me the difficulties of the past year for her and her boy. Her husband had passed and Brian was struggling with the recent loss. She referred to *The Karate Kid* as a constant source of joy and spoke of how many times the three of them had rewatched the film as a family. I saw a prompt in her eyes, that she had hopes I would engage with her son.

Like this was an opportunity for a special connection for him. This came as an unspoken request I picked up on fairly easily. Parental instinct, I guess.

I asked Brian what his favorite scenes were. At first, he kind of shrugged and shuffled his feet, perhaps a little embarrassed to dive into a forced conversation. Then I shared with him some of my favorite moments from the film. He became more engaged and excited as we went from the skeleton fight to the chores payoff scene to the final All Valley match. Before I knew it, he was smiling and asking questions. "Was Miyagi a cool guy in real life and do you still do karate?" Mom brought up his dad and how he would adapt lines from the movie around the house—"Always look eye, Brian-san," or "Fear does not exist in this kitchen." This seemed to loosen Brian up, and he laughed at these fond memories. He then offered a story about when he got a bike for his birthday and he and his dad had trouble getting the chain to stay on properly. They would impersonate LaRusso as he threw his bike into a dumpster, repeating, "I hate this bike, this stupid bike, I hate this bike!" I even did a mock version of it live right there for them, including rolling my eyes at my improvised overacted line reading, which had been forever captured on film.

As our collective laughter subsided, there was an announcement that my flight was boarding. It was time to part ways. I looked toward Mom and her eyes were brimming with tears. It was a powerful silent moment we shared. She mouthed, "Thank you," and I realized the gravity of our exchange and the fact that our short time together had been positive and maybe even impactful. For a few moments, the sun came out from behind the clouds. It may have been an experience·they would both always remember. As you can tell, I certainly have. I had a little Miyagi-mentor moment with a fatherless teen. Then a thought came to mind. I decided to reference the scene that followed the "I hate this bike" moment, where Daniel's mom came to the aid of her son, who was hurting and struggling. I shined a light on the importance of that mother-son relationship in the movie and told Brian that I thought his mom was awesome. It was probably the best thing I did during our encounter, because the look of gratitude that his mom gave to me is one that I haven't forgotten.

I gave Brian a high five and thanked him for being a fan, and I headed off toward my departure gate. I'm not exactly sure what city's airport this took place in, but my hope is that Brian and his mom are doing well and getting to enjoy *Cobra Kai* today. And that they are somehow aware of how fulfilling the experience was for me as well.

I remember the late Gene Siskel, the famous *Chicago Tribune* film critic and cohost of *Siskel & Ebert*, telling me how much he loved the mother-son relationship in *The Karate Kid*. How organic and real it felt to him. Ironically, it was Roger Ebert who gave the film four stars and a big thumbs-up. Siskel did not. It was thumbs-down, cliché and predictable in his eyes. However, he commented repeatedly on Randee Heller's work as Lucille LaRusso and our chemistry together, how it accurately captured the widowed mother and fatherless son dynamic.

I had met Randee Heller with John Avildsen in Bungalow One on the Columbia Pictures lot during pre-production on the film. She came in to read with me for her audition. There was instantaneous chemistry. It was evident and believable from our first interaction that these characters were family. Randee brought in the same East Coast sensibility that I had, and she was grounded and relatable from the start. If memory serves, she had to come back in a few times, as I think the studio and Weintraub wanted to investigate a "name actress" to play Lucille, even though it was clear to us we had already found her in Randee. Fortunately, Avildsen once again had his way and added another perfectly matched stroke of color to the casting canvas. Randee and I hit it off as actors and as friends. Behind the scenes we always loved to share opinions on music, movies, and acting. We were serious about the work and representing the characters accurately, but we also loved to playfully bullshit and laugh. We had a great time. And still do. Including Randee in *Cobra Kai* is always such a joy for the entire company. And on set, she and I still talk, sharing wide-ranging opinions and bullshitting and laughing like we did in years past.

All karate-kidding aside, much attention has been drawn to the father-and-son elements in both *The Karate Kid* and *Cobra Kai*. And that is fair and accurate. But I bring all of this up so we don't lose sight of the importance of the mom(s) in the story. Lucille LaRusso represented a strong woman in a relatable scenario, a single mother for whom starting a new life and carving a future for her son were paramount in the wake of their family tragedy. This is something we touch upon in season 4 of *Cobra Kai* as well. The writers do a beautiful job of connecting Daniel's relationship with his mom to his sharing his wisdom and experience with the Miguel Diaz character. Miguel has a similar fatherless dynamic with his mother, Carmen. It's the generational connective tissue that brings the heart and inspiration to the ongoing story.

My scenes with Randee in the original film were honest and authentic for a teenage boy and his mother navigating a new beginning. To that same point, having Lucille pop into *Cobra Kai* adds an element of groundedness to the LaRussos today. She shares her wisdom and sometimes ballsy opinions with Daniel and his wife, Amanda, the voice-of-reason character in the series. These two in-law moms will butt heads occasionally, with Daniel caught in the middle. Comedy ensues, and goose bumps are had with the lessons learned. It's always a highlight for me to play those scenes. They feel natural and organic. Well, maybe that's because they usually don't involve middle-aged kicking, punching, or ducking. Nevertheless, these strong female characters aim to guide and support Daniel LaRusso with much love and good intentions. Courtney Henggeler's performance as Amanda has evolved into an essential element in *Cobra Kai* and LaRusso's midlife journey. Their marriage and partnership grows deeper with each and every season. I have enjoyed developing that arc with her.

The power of mentoring is a component that lives and breathes on many levels in this franchise, Mr. Miyagi and Daniel clearly being the bedrock there. Whether the mentor is a surrogate father figure, mom, wife, or even former foe, mentorship is a primary theme that is woven into the fabric of the *Karate Kid* universe and the lore of Daniel LaRusso. And it's one that audiences have leaned into since the summer of 1984.

Bullying is an extremely complicated issue. Especially nowadays, with technology and social media at our fingertips. It's all more complex than ever. It has gone way beyond the schoolyard threats and the taking of lunch money that I remember as a kid. With that, I want to preface these following examples of the show's impact and inspiration with the disclaimer that I am in no way trivializing the issue, as it can be both deep-rooted and devastating, with a wide spectrum of severity. Bullying has always been a recurring theme of the *Karate Kid* franchise. Over the many years since the film's release, I have witnessed incalculable examples of fans offering me personal stories on how *The Karate Kid* played a part in their ability to cope and relate. Men and women, kids and teens, all of whom I have spoken to over the years about their struggles against various aspects of bullying.

"I Was Daniel LaRusso"

I can't begin to count the number of times someone has approached me with that line and then launched into their story. On certain occasions it would mirror the physical aspects of bullying that LaRusso experienced in the film. Various people I have met have explained how they chose to study martial arts specifically to combat the bullying in their lives, and that the self-defense they learned gave them the tools to confront and stand up to their foes. Some became black-belt level, and others got their whole families to embrace not only the physical but also the mental and spiritual philosophy as a way of life. These weren't just middle schoolers and teens. There were men and women with similar stories about how martial arts and the themes of *The Karate Kid* provided them with the guidance and inspiration to overcome their fears and obstacles in life. I often joke to this day that if I had a dollar for every karate class taken or bonsai tree purchased since June 22, 1984, I could have retired ten years ago.

On other occasions, the correlation to LaRusso is shared in a more internal way, more from a perspective of empowerment or the inspirational aspects of the character. One meaningful encounter that has always stuck with me was with a man I met who had Down syndrome. He referred to Daniel LaRusso as one of his best friends and said Daniel "makes him strong." His face was kind, his eyes were soulful. My guess would be he was in his early thirties. He was with his younger sister, who seemed to be very protective of him. I was walking around by myself at an outdoor mall when I heard "DanielLaRusso!" It was spoken a bit loudly and as if it was run together as one word. Sometimes I choose to ignore moments like this in public, but something about the enthusiasm and projection of this voice caused me to turn. His sister explained how much her brother loved the movie and that he watched it almost daily. I learned that his name was David, and I decided to sit down with both of them for a few minutes. David was beside-himself excited and soon addressed me as "Daniel-san," shedding the formality of DanielLaRusso as our conversation deepened and I spoke of how cool it was to meet him. The joy in his face and his love for what the movie represented to him were contagious.

His sister shared with me that when people would be mean and tease, he would always say he was strong like Daniel LaRusso, his best friend. I asked her to take a picture of us so they would have it to help them remember. We, all three of us, were as close to sharing pure joy in the moment as could be possible. David and I posed in a fighting stance together, fists up toward the phone camera. With big smiles, we both yelled, "Banzai!"—as a substitute for "cheese"—when taking the picture. It was his idea. I bade them farewell and I told him to be good to his sister and always find balance. He did his version of the crane stance as I stepped away and he called out, "Thank you, RalphMacchio!" I countered with "Thank *you*, David!" We waved as I turned the corner and that's pretty much where it ended.

Later that evening, as I was playing back the encounter in my mind, I was struck by a thought-provoking observation. David had addressed me by my character name at first, followed by the character's nickname, then ended it all by calling me by my real name. A progression from make-believe formal to personal and casual. I didn't want to give it more significance than it deserved, but from my perspective it felt good, and I was proud of that interaction. Once again, the impact and inspiration of Daniel LaRusso proved to be a two-way street.

I remember at a Comic-Con event, a young woman excitedly stepped up to me and spoke of her mentor. As a teen, her peers had ridiculed her, and her parents had never understood. No one did, until her English teacher became the Mr. Miyagi to her rudderless adolescence. She became emotional when recalling that time in her life. Having someone to help navigate the turbulent waters of high school bullying was invaluable. Feeling at one with a character who essentially had a similar story was comforting and empowering to her. She thanked me for *The Karate Kid* and its impression on her life. She vowed to pay it forward, as she was four months pregnant when she shared her story with me. Another life, or potentially two, that would be enhanced by this movie and its lead character.

There are far too many one-on-one examples to list, and they would only begin to mirror and repeat themselves regardless of how unique and special each is in its own way. So, I'll stop now and move into another area of inspiration.

Nowhere in the mainstream is wish fulfillment and motivation more dominantly showcased than in sports. I would imagine by now you will have drawn the conclusion that I am a sports fan. There has been some debate over the years on whether *The Karate Kid* is truly a sports movie. Some claim it's a fish-out-of-water movie about bullying with karate as a backdrop. Others say it is as much a sports movie as *Rocky*, which one can argue is really a love story with boxing as a backdrop. And the beat goes on. . . .

But does it inspire in the way of sports films like *Rudy* or *The Natural* or *Hoosiers*? After all, martial arts is not as mainstream as football or baseball or basketball. Or even hockey, in the case of the film *Miracle*, the story of the 1980 USA Olympic hockey team. Does *The Karate Kid* have the same sports impact as those listed? I can only tell you from my perspective what happens when I attend sporting events— whether one believes *The Karate Kid* is a sports movie or not. The impact is unwavering. I can speak firsthand to the fact that few characters pump up a crowd like Daniel LaRusso.

I was in attendance at game three of the 2015 World Series at Citi Field in New York. Mets vs. Royals. The Kansas City Royals wound up winning the championship that year in a pretty easy fashion. But there was a moment in game three that is noteworthy in regard to a movie character and live sporting events. The Mets were up 5–3 at that point, and in the sixth inning there was a feeling they might bust the game wide-open, essentially landing a knockout punch. A crane kick, if you will. There was a buzz in the sold-out crowd on that chilly October night, when I noticed a mobile camera-crew guy waving toward me. He was setting himself up down the row from where I was sitting, camera pointed in my direction. I had been in these situations before, so I knew what was coming. Up on the Jumbotron scoreboard, the movie clip of the moments before the climactic crane kick began, with Bill Conti's score building the anticipation. Immediately it seemed everyone in the stadium recognized the sound and image. Citi Field began to rumble in anticipation of LaRusso's "knockout punch." At once, the kick, the crescendo, the roar from the New York Mets faithful. And then the red light appeared on the camera and there I was up on the Jumbotron. A die-hard Mets fan at one with the people. A humbling cheer from the crowd led to a raucous "Let's go, Mets!" chant that carried the team to a four-run sixth inning and sealed the deal on World Series game three!

Now, neither *The Karate Kid* nor Daniel LaRusso nor I had absolutely anything to do with what happened on the field. That's for sure. However, I believe the connection with the crowd and the motivation in the moment boosted the fans' wish fulfillment. It was palpable and unmistakable. And just so much damn fun to be a part of. I am proud that I get to walk in those shoes. More recently, the same type of scenario occurred at almost every New York Islanders Stanley Cup semifinals game in 2021. The fact that *Cobra Kai* is current only added to the thunder from the crowd of all ages; the audience is even wider today with the show's Netflix presence. The in-game presentation producers put up an image of present-day LaRusso on the scoreboard with the caption "Wax-On Play-Offs." Underneath the image was an animated "Get Loud" meter prompting the crowd to move the needle. There was my LaRusso face again, up on the Jumbotron. Towels waved and fans cheered to break a tie in the third or hold the lead or send the game to overtime. It's a typical but wonderful sports story, cheering the underdog on to victory. And this is not only exclusive to in-game fan experiences. Earlier in that same hockey season, the Washington Capitals coach would award a Miyagi-Do headband to the defensive player of the game. He then, in turn, would offer a Cobra Kai headband to the offensive player of the game. This happened for the entire season as a motivating gesture for these professional athletes. Whether it's the reporter referencing Rafael Nadal at the US Open in his headband as Karate Kid–like or the Fox Sports robot on an NFL game doing the crane into the commercial break, *The Karate Kid* still inspires in the sporting world, and its impact is here to stay.

There are certainly other examples in storytelling of characters who serve as role models who inspire and are impactful. But few reach such a wide range of ages and genders so effectively. It's sort of universal, across the board and around the world. I believe that is rare. To encourage self-esteem and confidence at any level. To stimulate overcoming obstacles and impart the wisdom of its philosophy. Robert Kamen truly wrote a timeless script with compelling and memorable characters. The lessons and themes of *The Karate Kid* are referenced in schoolrooms and in workplaces. They have been incorporated into religious homilies and victory speeches.

The film is a prime example of when Hollywood gets it all right. It teaches and inspires through pure entertainment. Sure, the cynics can call it the silly popcorn karate movie that it is. And that's fair enough. But the human elements beneath all of that and the impact on the world's audience will never cease to inspire me in my life. And what a wonderful gift that is.

CHAPTER TEN

Finding Balance

A very ambitious shooting day sat in front of us as we were getting toward the end of production on *The Karate Kid*. It was mid-December and it was quite cool in the early morning, though the daytime temperature would later rise to the upper seventies. The location was a reservoir way north in the San Fernando Valley, or perhaps even farther north than there. My memory of the exact geographical location is a bit fuzzy. However, the experience of the day's accomplishments is still crystal clear in my mind. The moments that were captured on that day included a few of my personal favorites. We had a full agenda and needed to get everything in the can before dark. And with winter approaching, dark came a lot earlier. Our work was cut out for us. Early that morning, I dipped my toe in the water only to find it was unexpectedly cold. I imagine the night air dropping down to the forties outmuscled the seventy-degree average daytime temperature. My impending fate was swirling around my frontal lobes. I knew I would be hitting that water at some point in the next few hours. It was a chilly consideration that I forced to the back of my mind as our first scene of the day approached. *Focus, Daniel-san.*

The first scene was the one where Daniel was to balance on the bow of Mr. Miyagi's rowboat while his mentor tossed out his fishing line in addition to his profound wisdom. LaRusso would practice his blocks, and the dynamic duo would have a poignant father-and-son-type exchange about the importance of balance in life. The scene concludes with the feisty and impatient LaRusso ending up in the water after pushing the issue about wanting to learn how to punch. The second sequence we shot that day is one of the most beautifully photographed montage moments in the movie. We discover Daniel training himself on the bow of the boat at magic hour. The camera glides along the glistening lake, holding the frame in a long shot as Daniel practices his moves in cinematic solitude. Bill Conti's gorgeously orchestrated "Training Hard" underscores the silhouetted image. It still gives me chills every time. The final scene of the day was Daniel's "learning how to punch" sequence, with Mr. Miyagi in a baseball catcher's mask and chest protector. A scene that was lightly scripted, with the choreography improvised as the sun quickly disappeared behind the surrounding mountain-scape. All three pieces, though different, cinematic, funny, heartfelt, and inspiring, had one thing in common. . . .

Balance

There was a lot of teasing going on earlier in the day from Pat, Avildsen, and the entire crew, because everyone knew I was stressing about how cold the water was going to be. The playful tension was mounting. I vowed to do it in one take and one take only. We made sure we got all of the dialogue completed and covered from all angles before the inevitable dunk happened. Pat took pleasure in daring me to not fall in before I had to, occasionally dipping and jarring the boat in between takes to see if he could catch me off guard. No matter how hard he tried, I kept my skinny legs engaged like nimble shock absorbers. I would not be denied. Morita couldn't get Macchio to lose his balance. However, when it was time, Mr. Miyagi prevailed over Daniel-san. *Splash!* If you review that moment after I climb back into the boat, you can see both of us laughing and trying to cover it. It was a genuinely honest moment between actors and friends. I remember Avildsen commenting that I came up and out quicker than I fell in. I was back in the boat speedier than the Looney Tunes Road Runner and he wasn't sure how I even got wet. He claimed he needed to see the developed film first to confirm we'd gotten what we needed and ribbed me that we might have to come back and do it again. Nuh-uh. It worked in one. And yes, it was damn cold!

The importance of finding balance was touched upon in a few areas with that scene. Wise nuggets of information passed from teacher to student. It is one of those quintessential *Karate Kid* signatures. In the magic-hour montage that followed, balance was featured through LaRusso's mastering of the defensive moves he had learned as he centered himself in anticipation of the upcoming All Valley tournament. The final scene on that shooting day tilted toward losing balance, when getting ahead of yourself blurs your focus and leads to your being taken down in a vulnerable moment. A little comeuppance for the kid who was being too cocky.

Every fan knows that at the core of Daniel LaRusso's training is the concept of finding balance. It's what separated his character from the bullies and misfits. It is spotlighted in the film's clear messaging as to why he triumphed in the end. I never expected those same lessons would be as influential in my own life when I was making the film. I have been blessed more than once in regard to my own personal triumphs, and I would have to credit balance as the reason for at least some of those victories. Perhaps the subconscious Miyagi-isms were germinating in my young mind and eventually yielded some of the fruits. Somehow this Karate Kid kept on teaching me, and the lessons continue even now.

I have often described my recipe for avoiding the pitfalls of show business as keeping "one foot in and one foot out." Essentially, finding the balance in life and work and family. I believe this has grounded me for whatever reason, though it hasn't always been easy or without certain repercussions. At least on the career side. Few would dispute that finding balance is an important component in living a successful and healthy life. A balanced family. A balanced marriage. A balanced career.

A balanced diet. And so on. It definitely comes with its challenges, and often the need to restrain oneself from what can be seductive. However, I have always looked to safely navigate these sometimes-turbulent waters, striving to locate the central balance point and keep from ever tipping over too far.

Now, I don't have the crash-and-burn-to-redemption story many of these types of memoirs produce, or that sometimes become the main incentive for writing a memoir. Any fall from grace I experienced was not due to drug addiction, crime, or flagrant misbehavior. Nope. Sorry. Wrong guy here. I skew more toward the anti–*E! True Hollywood Story*. But there were a few areas of note that required me to do some realigning and balancing to get through successfully. Times in my life and career when things were challenging and I may have been less than focused on finding a healthy solution. Or, at the least, a better way to deal. Times when I became frustrated and angry with the limitations in my career and how that would put undue strain on my marriage and family. Where I would waffle, discouraged, trapped in limbo as opposed to being proactive. Or I was afraid that the "wrong" decision would backfire. Areas where balanced choices were often my saving grace, even if it didn't seem that way at the outset. It's really quite remarkable how many pieces of wisdom were born out of Robert Kamen's creation of Mr. Miyagi and his life lessons. I dare anyone to deny that they apply to almost everybody at some point in their life.

Walk on road.
Walk right side, safe.
Walk left side, safe.
Walk middle, sooner or later,
you get squished, just like grape.

I am always asked what is my favorite Miyagi lesson or piece of advice that I would use or have already applied to my own life. There are a few that I have retained, but I would have to say the above is the one that I probably preach most and that I have used as advice for myself and my own family. It is pulled from the scene in Mr. Miyagi's front yard where he first instructs Daniel-san as he begins his training. The concept here is that the only bad choice is no choice. That you should, instead, follow what you instinctively believe while being true to yourself. This way any repercussions that you may have to deal with come from a place of honesty and a direction that you have chosen from your gut. It's more comforting to roll with any obstacles or missteps knowing that you didn't wobble rudderless down the middle.

I believe in owning one's choices, whether good or bad. When I think of how everything has worked out for me in regard to balancing my family and career, it may look like I played it perfectly. But once again, *not everything is as seem*. It may only look as if I played it perfectly. Especially now, in particular, with how well received *Cobra Kai* has been by fans, critics, and the industry alike. Good things come to those who wait? Well, in my case, luck and good fortune had a big hand in it. Though many say that you do create your own luck. Either way, here's a story from a time when I did not possess focus or balance. Where I was almost "squished, just like grape."

My daughter, Julia, was probably around two years old, singing, dancing, and playacting to/with Barney the dinosaur on a daily basis. Today, she is an amazing professional dancer, singer, and actress. "Do as I say, not as I do" did not succeed. LOL. But back when she was a toddler, I was mostly out of work. My wife, Phyllis, a nurse practitioner, was preparing for the birth of our second child. My son, Daniel, was born a little over a year after that. Yes, we named our son Daniel. There was a big back-and-forth about whether that would be the right move. My wife always wanted to name a son Daniel, after her cousin, who was her closest friend growing up and throughout her life, and of course we know of the name's influence on my life. It had a twofold meaning and significance to us both, and that is why we chose it. My son, now an adult in his midtwenties, goes by Dan these days. Though we'll always remember and recall certain childhood occurrences, like a Little League game when he tripped rounding third base and the opposing coach shouted, "DOWN goes LaRusso!" Dusting himself off, my son eyed me with a look that said, *Really, Dad? Thanks, thanks a lot.* We all smile at those memories today.

Returning to the story, back before Dan was born, we were planning the growth of our family on Long Island, since at that point, my career had little to no growth of its own. The future was looming and unknown, and the unknown was daunting to me. This was the early 1990s. *My Cousin Vinny* had come and gone. I was grappling with how I was going to provide for my family. I was far away from Hollywood. Movies had dried up for me, with the exception of smaller independent films that barely paid the union minimum. They might have fed the soul, but they in no way fed the pocketbook.

My agents, who for the most part I rarely heard from, presented me with the concept of considering a broadcast television series. This was at a time when actors were in two separate categories, those who would do TV and those who wouldn't. *Really? Harrison Ford would never do a sitcom; why would I?* It makes me laugh when I consider that was my inner response, considering that today we are in the golden age of television, where some of the best writing and most complex characters come out of TV. That line has been completely blurred. There is no stigma attached to doing TV anymore. Great storytelling is great storytelling, be it a theatrical film or a television series. But my ego was getting in the way and I was feeling the pressure. I did not know what I wanted. I was hovering in the middle.

I knuckled under in my desperation to try to make things fit, and I took meetings in Los Angeles with TV production studios. In retrospect, it was a positive opportunity, but I instead looked at it as a glass-half-empty scenario. That was the real issue—I was holding on to the past instead of embracing the future. I landed a development deal at a major studio to try to find a series project that would be a fit. This would be considered a win by all accounts. But for me, it took me away from home without knowing what the project might be and whether it would even be in an area I was comfortable with. And if it all worked, I would potentially have to relocate to Los Angeles. My wife had given it her blessing, but for me, it was a lot to sift through. Both my family and my work suffered from my inability to commit fully to either. And that part was on me. My life was back in New York. I had both feet in Hollywood, but neither was on solid ground. Nothing was firmly planted. I would describe this fairly short window in my life as "both feet out."

The development deal did wind up yielding a few episodes of a series; however, it never went anywhere. And what followed from there was the first (and thankfully last) time my work reputation was tarnished by my inability to fully engage in my choices. Still, once you are in a development deal, very often your choices aren't yours. They become the wishes of the buyer, meaning the studio or network. And the more I felt that manipulation away from having healthy collaboration or a voice, the further I sank into frustration. It was a novice play on my part because I never attempted to make lemonade out of the lemons. And that was unlike me.

The eye-opening moment came when I had back-to-back phone calls in my hotel room in Los Angeles, one with my wife, who was home in New York with my daughter, and the other with my TV agent at the time. They were both asking me essentially the same question. Each was looking for guidance from me from two totally different perspectives. Both my career and my family were suffering in my absence. And the mirrored question was simple: What do you want? Or more pointedly, what are your plans? And it was in that moment, as the one-two punch in the stomach landed, that I realized I had no definitive answer for either. I was stuck in the middle of the road. And I wasn't being truthful to myself in either section of my life at the time. I knew I needed to be close to my young family. If I wasn't, I needed to find creative work that inspired me. And if it was about money, then I'd need to figure that out separately. I had to recalibrate and realign myself with one foot in and one foot out when I needed it to be. That's what worked for me in my case. Even if it meant being away from the spotlight for a while.

It was never wholly by design, how success wound up working out for me. Or shall I say, it exceeded expectations and it has been just shy of an embarrassment of riches when I look at where I stand in 2022. So, I'll go with the theory that you make your own luck. I am very grateful for mine. The fact that this TV project never got off the ground back then was a blessing in disguise. When I got word that the network didn't want any more episodes, there was a short beat of disappointment followed by a long moment of relief. I needed to refocus and rediscover the balance in my life. So, in a way, this was a great gain out of the lost opportunity. I don't always agree with the idea that things happen for a reason, but in this case, it was all for the right reason.

As an interesting footnote to this story, both the smash hit *Friends* and the equally popular *ER* came out of that development season at the same studio. They each premiered in the fall of 1994 while I was on another series from the same studio for the same network. We made six episodes that still have never seen the light of day. I'm sure they live somewhere in a vault on deteriorating VHS tapes. They say don't look back. Fall forward, right? And that's what I did. The experience wound up putting balance back into my life. But could you imagine? *Joey Tribbiani? Dr. Carter?* Nah, I needed this journey to inform my choices going forward so as not to lose balance or get squished on the next one. That experience led me back to once again discovering the sweetness in the lemonade. Perhaps with the slightest hint of grape.

In the years that followed, I became more focused on writing screenplays and making short films. I had great success with my Sundance short *Love Thy Brother*, and I began to plant seeds and network in the area of filmmaking. Another film I wrote and directed, *Across Grace Alley*, came after that. I would draw from the lessons that I had learned from the Avildsens and Coppolas of the world. I kept myself creatively fulfilled and thriving during those leaner acting years. I was finding the balance in work and family. Not always easy or exactly where I wanted it to be from a career perspective, but I was in a solid place.

I am a family man. That's who I am. That's where my roots are. From my upbringing through present day. If you ask most people around me, I believe they would say that my wife and kids are my favorite subject. Okay, at least when I'm not talking about myself. Haha. And I would say that the "school of parenting" is the most humbling in all of life. I slip and fall constantly, but each time I try to learn a little bit along the way. It's the job I'm most proud of. I often express that I am lucky that I have such amazing kids. And without hesitation, I also follow with "They are lucky too," shining a favorable light on my wife and myself as parents. We are, all four of us, very close.

"It's okay to lose to opponent. Must not lose to fear."

There is a story line in *Cobra Kai* season 3 that is worth noting here. It is one that focuses on deep anxiety and the consequences of bullying. A story point in that season of the series mirrors certain scenes in my parenting life. I had an experience with my own daughter, Julia, that I was able to incorporate into the scenes with LaRusso's daughter, Samantha, played by Mary Mouser. I'm happy to say that Julia and Mary have become friends over the course of the series. They have called each other "sista from the same mista." It's an unexpected highlight for me, how much my kids connect with the young *Cobra Kai* cast.

We are an extended family on and off the stages, and that has been a personal joy to witness. Who knew that such a big part of my younger life would be such a relevant part of my kids' lives today? I can only describe this as special.

In the specific *Cobra Kai* story line, Samantha has been struggling with intense anxiety over being bullied by her nemesis in the show. It has crippling effects in her life and comes to the surface on a day out with her dad, yours truly. (Quick sidebar: Mary and I shot all of those scenes together on my birthday in 2019. It was a most excellent day at the office.) I bring up this example as it is another area where the theme of finding balance and passing on what I've learned resonates with me on a personal level. In this instance, offering wisdom through experience as a parent. Our first scene took place out on a rowboat, a callback to the balance boat scene in *The Karate Kid* I wrote about earlier in this chapter. Samantha is succumbing to fear in her life back at school and finds herself paralyzed with anxiety. LaRusso at first doesn't read the signals, but as the truth reveals itself, it opens up an awareness and recollection of his own past experience. A revelation. He applies this parenting tool to connect with Samantha with understanding, coming from a place of "you are not alone and you never need to be alone." He put himself on the same plane as her, having gone through similar episodes in his life—essentially, having walked in her shoes.

I had a comparable scenario with Julia years back when she was experiencing bullying in middle school. I too didn't read the signals at first. My wife was way ahead of me on that. And I had a few missteps at the outset before I shared some of my own insecurities growing up, revealing anxieties that I had dealt with as the youngest-looking and skinniest kid in my class, how inferior I had felt when being teased or picked on. I then transitioned to today and the adult concerns I deal with in life as I look to keep my feet firmly planted. Placing father and daughter on the same level became positive and a comfort to both Julia and me.

I shared those experiences with Mary, and it helped us build those scenes together and communicate the overall psychology of leveling off the wings in flight and finding a balance together. When you are centered and on solid ground, you have a better chance of dealing with anything. Even the fear of the unknown. This is not intended to preach or pretend that there's an easy fix to bullying or anxiety. I am not trivializing the challenges and difficulty in the real world. I only offer these thoughts as an invitation to explore. For me, the biggest mistakes in my life have come when I surrendered to fear. This is wisdom I always attempt to instill and pay forward. It is a parallel theme layered into *The Karate Kid*. I take it to heart and choose to simply see it as another shiny pearl gifted from the Miyagiverse.

Incidentally, Julia appears in episode 408 of *Cobra Kai*. She plays Vanessa, a strong-minded member of the LaRusso family. A feisty character who questions LaRusso's parenting skills. What a blast it was for everyone to have her on the show, and what a unique joy this was for me. Though maybe not nearly as much fun as it was for the writing staff. They had a field day with the meta concept of casting my own kid to point out her dad's shortcomings as a parent. They took distinct pleasure in that. And I tipped my hat with a wry smile.

"First learn stand, then learn fly."

I remember seeing an interview with the late Christopher Reeve in which he referenced the importance of "roots and wings." It made an impression on me at the time. I recall thinking it through and connecting it as a piece of advice in my life. This was before I had children. So, it was easy to conceptualize and not so easy to apply when it was in front of me. Reeve was speaking of his parents and their ability to employ that theory in raising him. That time in parental life when you make sure to secure the foundation before you need to let go. The bonsai tree references in *The Karate Kid*, and *Cobra Kai*, for that matter, carry on that messaging. Strong roots allow for the tree to grow healthy and in any direction it chooses. This is a philosophy that I try to echo in my life. Though I found it difficult to "let go," especially when it came to my kids. However, I recognize its importance. The importance of discovering your own way, learning to navigate the path on your own. Whether it's on the bow of the boat or the balance board in Miyagi's backyard, these life lessons are instilled into the franchise. Essential training for a healthy mind, body, and soul. Laced into story lines and character speeches from the *Karate Kid* universe.

And it is in the present day and current times that I have the opportunity to continue to mentor these ideals and theories. In *Cobra Kai*, LaRusso offers his seasoned insights to the next generation. He carries on the teachings of his mentor. And out on the street, as a father, husband, and friend, I myself aim to use these tools to remain centered in all facets of life, never tipping too far in one direction. Life imitates art as art imitates life. Once again, the line is blurred between Macchio and LaRusso. Yet somehow it always remains clear to us both . . .

Whole life have balance. Everything be better.
—MR. MIYAGI

CHAPTER ELEVEN

Do-Overs

I'm not a fan of focusing on regrets. However, even though I'm quite proud of how I stuck the landing, looking back, there are some things I would have played differently, and there's advice I would have given my younger self. Those times when I was shortsighted or bitter that everything wasn't going the way I had planned. Or maybe I was not as dialed in as I could have been when making a choice. Life is not a dress rehearsal, they say. Sometimes you're not afforded a second take. And if you do get one, well, then you may possibly have a shot at redemption. But most of the time it evaporates without a chance for a redo. The opportunity disappears, and down the road you find yourself running on empty, looking for a do-over. It's happened to me in rare cases surrounding *The Karate Kid*. Not very often, but enough that these instances remain stamped into my memory.

I have carefully placed a few words in the previous paragraph that segue into this first experience. A slightly clever if not blatant foreshadowing of where I'm going with this story.

One of my favorite filmmakers of the late sixties, seventies, and eighties was the great Sidney Lumet. His films included multiple Academy Award nominees and winners, like *Network*, *Dog Day Afternoon*, *12 Angry Men*, *Serpico*, and *The Verdict*, just to name a few. He directed many of my acting heroes when I was growing up, and his films remain some of my top picks to date. That era of seventies moviemaking is still unrivaled, in my view.

Back in 1986, after a performance of *Cuba and His Teddy Bear* on Broadway, I was told by my co-star Robert De Niro (another of those abovementioned acting heroes) that Mr. Lumet was in the audience that particular evening. And he was going to stop backstage to see us. Well, you can imagine my excitement upon hearing this news. I will say this much: When you're co-starring with De Niro on Broadway, you get to meet a lot of amazing people. And this was certainly the case with my run in *Cuba*.

Sidney Lumet knocked on my dressing room door at the Longacre Theatre. I readied myself as I had when other legendary filmmakers, like Martin Scorsese and Elia Kazan, visited De Niro earlier in the run. As a young actor, this was so cool I can't even begin to explain it. I felt I'd had a solid show that night and opened the door with eager anticipation. Lumet had a New York grit to him, yet he spoke with an articulate rasp. His thoughtful compliments on my performance had me at hello. There was a mutual respect and I was over the moon. It was a brief encounter, maybe five minutes at most.

But it ended with his mentioning a film he was planning to make. He was interested in having me play a significant role in the movie. That film's title was *Running on Empty*. The actor who eventually played that role was River Phoenix. And he was nominated for an Academy Award as Best Supporting Actor. It was a well-deserved achievement for a gifted actor who left the world way too soon. I will stand by my "right actor, right part" theory. The nomination proves that to be true once again. But this was a tough one, as I often wondered, *What if?*

Cutting to the chase, what happened was, the slot for Lumet to make *Running on Empty* for Warner Bros. wound up being at the same time Columbia Pictures had scheduled production for *The Karate Kid Part III*. Conversations went back and forth, but at the end of the day, I was under contract to make the second sequel and my option was picked up. The *Running on Empty* ship was about to sail, and I was consigned back to my original port of call. To say that I felt frustrated would be an understatement. I wanted the cake and to eat it too. I felt I needed a dramatic film role to balance the commercial success of the *Karate Kid* franchise. When all was said and done, I don't think the production schedules wound up exactly conflicting with each other. But by that point, River Phoenix had won the role rightfully. All was well with Lumet and me. We continued on a few other occasions to try to find a project to work on together, but it never did happen. But as far as my encounters and discussions with Mr. Lumet, all was peachy. He was one of the greats. I was thrilled he thought that highly of me. I took pride in that and still do. No need for a do-over there.

That was all merely the setup for what happened next. The following is more on point with the concept of wanting another crack at something. It took place in the wake of *The Karate Kid Part III* option pickup and the blocking out of other opportunities like *Running on Empty*. I was bitter. I was frustrated. I was over it. And then into my dressing room at the Longacre Theatre walked another Oscar-winning filmmaker, a true movie star by the name of Warren Beatty.

With the bad taste still lingering in my mouth, I started to talk, and Mr. Beatty became a sounding board of sorts. A role I'm sure he didn't think he would have to play on that particular day. This was after a Sunday matinee performance. He sauntered into my dressing room oozing that aura of, well, I mean, it was Warren Beatty. . . . Hollywood royalty, right? He immediately put out his hand and introduced himself. We spoke about the play for a beat and he congratulated me on the run. But what he put the most emphasis on was the success of *The Karate Kid* and *Part II*, which was in theaters at that time. He complimented me on Daniel LaRusso and spoke to the themes and story of the movie. Specifically, the impact of a role like that. I shrugged it off by downplaying his compliment with a fair amount of pessimism toward the franchise and the typecasting that was beginning to creep up on me. I kept trying to spin the conversation back to the play. A role that I was hoping to re-create on film someday, since the dramatic depth of the Teddy character could provide a counterpoint to *The Karate Kid*'s dominance. In the play, De Niro played a Cuban American drug dealer and I his artistic-minded son, a writer, who was experimenting with heroin. A very different dynamic and tone from *The Karate Kid*. (De Niro did have a screenplay written, and we had discussed taping a performance for HBO; however, neither ever materialized.)

Upon hearing my discontentment, Beatty took it upon himself to have a seat. If only I had seen the significance of this gesture at the time. Youth is wasted on the young. He attempted to explain to me how the industry works. "Don't you . . . don't look down on those movies," he said carefully. "You need that as much as you want this" (meaning the De Niro play). He was reaching out to this cocky young actor with his experience and offering a fresh viewpoint to embrace. At the time, I was too clouded by ego and frustration to see the clear perspective. I had no idea what the story would be for the second *Karate Kid* sequel. So it wasn't that I knew what it was and didn't like it. I was just opposed to doing something again that I had already accomplished (twice) successfully. I wanted to grow with other opportunities. And the binding contract and imminent typecasting were hindering those potential opportunities.

I went on to him about the commercial aspects and desiring more artistic expression and a less linear type of entertainment. I think he understood what I meant, especially since he'd succeeded on each side of the camera during his illustrious career. But I'm sure I came off as spoiled or even bratty. I was not fully absorbing his words of wisdom as he tried to explain that one can help and balance the other. He still took his time with me as he advised me further, and I did finally ease off from my initial defensiveness. He held my gaze to make sure I was receiving what he was saying. There was a brief moment when I felt like I was in *Heaven Can Wait* (the greatest "body-switching" movie of all time, IMHO) when his character was trying to reach his closest friend, who didn't recognize him, and earnestly pleaded, "Can't you see me, Max? It's Joe Pendleton . . . come on, Max." Later, upon recollection, his words would echo in my ear as "You hear me, kid? It's me, Warren Beatty . . . come on, Ralph."

On the day, I probably took away about half of what he was saying, as I was filtering only what I wanted to hear. But as time went on in both my life and my career, his messaging became crystal clear. The proof is in how I carry myself now. But that day, as my brief time with Mr. Beatty came to an end, I thanked him for stopping by and hanging for a bit. I don't think I ever mentioned all of the movies that he had made that I loved. I was such a fan, and I regret that I was so self-absorbed during our discussion. He smiled and patted me on the shoulder as he left, offering a "Good luck" on his way out.

In the months following, I played this encounter over in my mind, hoping that my behavior hadn't overshadowed my respect for the legendary movie star/filmmaker. I deliberated about what he must have thought and generally just hoped for the best. I wonder if he has knowledge of *Cobra Kai* and of how I now represent myself in regard to the continued blessing of playing this character and the legacy that I cherish. Who knows? I guess I can only say that I hope he does. It still bothers me, how I presented myself in that moment. It may seem small in retrospect, and I might have inflated the reality over time, but I'd surely take a do-over on that one.

As an actor, in almost every film performance, there's at least one scene or moment you want back, to grab another shot at nailing it. On the theater stage, you often have the next curtain time to improve upon the previous performance. But on film, once it's in the can, it lives as is. It is often difficult to be objective while watching one's own work on the screen. Sometimes even the scenes that play beautifully for the audience are challenging to watch when it's you who is up there. And you don't want to dim the lantern on a moment or a scene that may taint another's opinion of it. But there is one scene in *The Karate Kid*—or actually one speech in a noted scene—where I have always felt I came up short. And as I've looked back on it, my feelings haven't changed. I would have loved to do it over and improve upon it if I could. Now, before I delve into which scene this was, I want to note that this is a personal opinion, and I am not looking to undermine anyone who may disagree with me. I know I run the risk of now putting a label on something in the film that you may have no issues with, or possibly place a dark cloud over a beloved moment. But I have to be honest: There is one piece, one passage of dialogue, in the original film that I wish I had another chance at. And by this time in the book, especially in a chapter with this title, it feels like the perfect place to expand on that.

LaRusso is lying on an exam table in the locker room at the All Valley. His knee has been injured by a blatantly illegal strike from Bobby of the Cobra Kai. He can't compete in the final match. Or so we think. He is crushed. His mom, Lucille, and girlfriend, Ali, exit the locker room, followed by Mr. Miyagi. Daniel stops his mentor. He asks Mr. Miyagi if he thought he had a chance at winning while pleading with Miyagi to fix his leg. Miyagi explains there is no need to fight anymore. This prompts a speech from Daniel-san about the worth of balance and why he needs to get back out there. He is devastated and feels he let everyone down.

It is in this speech that I feel I missed the bull's-eye, or wish I had been able to take a deeper dive into mining those emotions. I know Avildsen was looking for more too. He was pushing me to go further. I believe I had it in rehearsals, but on the shooting day the level felt a little manufactured, as opposed to organic and real emotional hurt. I know John was looking for LaRusso to break down, but the tears weren't happening in an organic way. It was frustrating me that I couldn't get the waterworks flowing, so I wound up playing the frustration. That, in the end, was the direction of the performance. Most often it's a better choice than faking it. I mean, the scene worked, and it plays well, but it never "got there" for me. In baseball terms, I hit a solid double, maybe even stretched that speech into a triple. But it was not the home run it could have been. In the final cut of that scene, the camera angle is across me and on Pat Morita for most of the speech. I have always felt if I truly nailed it, Avildsen would have played it more on my close-up. And that sits with me every time I see it. In a performance that otherwise fills me with pride, that's my one personal shortcoming.

The moment that immediately follows, when Mr. Miyagi says, "Close eye," and LaRusso realizes that his mentor will in fact work his magic on the injured knee . . . Well, there I was back on track. That's a moment I feel I crushed, with the wide-eyed, hopeful expression of a young heroic protagonist. Ah, victory supported by some cinematic wonderment. A thunderous hand clap, with the anticipation heightened by the music of the maestro Conti. Miyagi's hands vigorously rubbing together, ready to administer the Okinawan elixir! Then we cut to the tournament arena for . . .

"Daniel LaRusso's gonna fight?

"Daniel LaRusso's gonna FIGHT!!"

And the rest is crane kick climax history. . . .

———

Getting to play *The Karate Kid* callback scenes in *Cobra Kai* is a unique joy, not to mention a personal chance for a shot at redemption in the few places where I might need it. Jon, Josh, and Hayden instinctively know how and when to turn a classic moment on its ear and make it fresh and new. They're always searching every nook and cranny of the franchise to cleverly layer the comedic and the dramatic into *Cobra Kai* with heartfelt respect for *The Karate Kid*. In the case of the locker room scene, I had the opportunity to revisit it, so to speak. Only now it was from the mentor's side. In season 1 of the show, Robby (Johnny's son/Daniel's student) has his shoulder injured during the tournament, just as Daniel's leg was injured in the movie. This leads to a teacher-student exchange with a speech about rivalry, fatherhood, and acceptance. A speech that I am extremely proud of and one in which I connected deeply with Tanner Buchanan (Robby). He wore the Daniel-san shoes, and I was standing in the footprints of Mr. Miyagi. I offered LaRusso's interpretation of Miyagi mentorship, and it was one of the more grounded scenes I had in all of *Cobra Kai* season 1. Thanks to some wonderful writing and a talented screen partner, I got to dial it in from another vantage point. And happily, I felt no need for a do-over this time. The comedic twist came when LaRusso rubbed his hands together in anticipation of creating some of his own Miyagi magic, only to call out, "MEDIC!" Book-ended a few seconds later with *Daniel LaRusso's gonna coach? Daniel LaRusso's gonna COACH!!* I thought it might have been too much when we shot it. But the fans ate it up!

F or all of the great things I believe I did right, here is one mistake that bothers me the most. It sat somewhere be-tween the theatrical release of *Teachers* and the early prepping of *Crossroads*. That is when my biggest *Karate Kid*–related "mess-up" happened. Boy, do I wish I could have this one back. The good news—the silver lining, if you will—is that years after the event took place, I was able to redeem myself to a satisfying end. But from where I sit today, my original decision back then goes against virtually everything I would advise now. In the spring of 1985, my focus was hazy. My viewpoint was distorted. The right thing to do didn't line up with my young, rebellious thinking. And for lack of a better description, it was a self-proclaimed stupid choice for no good reason.

I was in the family room of my house on Long Island when the phone rang. I was getting used to life as a "famous person," which was now the new normal. The popularity of *The Karate Kid* was growing and I was a little overwhelmed by it all. I preferred to lie a bit low at that time, staying close to home while pulling *out* the one foot that had been *in* for a while. I made a rash decision and chose to pass on a grand opportunity. I was looking to separate myself from the pigeonholing that was beginning to happen; it was looming in my mind. This indeed may prove to have been a once-in-a-lifetime opportunity, considering that to this very day it has not presented itself again. In fairness, my reps at the time did not attempt to persuade me otherwise or make a strong argument against my decision. Perhaps they were just catering to the client. But I wish they had taken a stance against my short-sighted instincts. I don't recall every aspect in the decision-making, as some of the details are fuzzy, but that doesn't change the result. In the end it was my choice, and I own it. I picked up the phone and I received the news. . . .

"You have been invited to present at the Oscars alongside Pat Morita."

And I passed. . . .

This one hurts the most, as Pat was also nominated for Best Supporting Actor and I did not attend the ceremony. I mean, that's a bad job right there. Somehow, I brushed it off. The weight and significance were lost on me in my ignorant youth. I was too focused on distancing myself and whatever else I prioritized at that age. I was buried in my daily home life and made a hasty decision. I let it go. I moved on. Until it was Oscar night.

I was in the same family room where I'd received the invitation call. It was me, my girlfriend (now wife), Phyllis, and my parents, Ralph Sr. and Rosalie. We had one of the earlier big-screen eighties front-projection TVs. The console held three lights (red, green, blue) that would bounce the image up onto the fifty-inch screen. It was a blurry picture by today's 4K standards, but we were the cool family that had one. My dad always went for the latest when it came to that stuff. The bigger we could see the Mets, Islanders, or *All in the Family* reruns, the better! We probably had some popcorn or Entenmann's chocolate-covered donuts and we were getting ready for the ceremony to begin. Show-business peers would often tell me what a stressful circus of a day it is at the Academy Awards, so I was happy to be lounging in my jeans, T-shirt, and sweat socks. I was sitting back and I was chill.

Until the moment came when I saw Pat on camera. I felt an immediate shift in perspective. Specifically, when clips of *The Karate Kid* were shown—I had the sinking feeling that I had made a mistake. And it sucked. I blew it. I should have been there supporting and sharing in those privileged moments. This was our movie and I had chosen not to represent it. And I knew in an instant. I never verbalized it or shared it with my parents or Phyllis. I kept it to myself and we watched the show. We were rooting for Pat to get the trophy as I was battling a sour stomach due to my blunder. Incidentally, Haing S. Ngor won in Pat's category for his devastatingly authentic performance in *The Killing Fields*. But few can dispute the staying power of Pat's Mr. Miyagi in cinema history. He was a winner that night and always will be.

I remember a quote I gave back in the eighties that still makes me shake my head. It went something like "My plan is to work until I am about thirty years old and then kick back and enjoy life." I mean, the arrogance of youth. Who says that? Who even thinks that? This must be where the ill-advised logic came from with the Oscar-presenting decision—the concept that I had a blank page to write on and I'd just get another chance when I wanted. The opposite of seizing the opportunity when it presented itself. Well, fortunately for me, I did get another grand opportunity, albeit not at the Academy Awards.

I never really spoke to Pat about my 1985 Oscars misstep, so I wasn't sure if it was an issue for him. He never let on that it was. Our friendship was consistent even when we were out of touch during certain eras. It was always welcoming and positive, highlighted with laughs and love and respect. But my disappointment in myself always hung in the back of my mind.

Decades later, I received another phone call, this time on my cell phone, not the family room rotary-dial. It was from the lead producer of the Asian Excellence Awards, regarding a formal concert event to be held at Lincoln Center in New York City. They were honoring Pat Morita with a lifetime achievement award. They told me Pat had specifically requested that I be the one to present him with this prestigious award. I jumped at this opportunity—I believe I said yes before they finished the question. This was my chance at personal redemption, and I took it. I hadn't seen Pat in a couple of years, so this would prove to be a mini-reunion of sorts. We hadn't been in public, let alone onstage together, in probably ten years at that time. I had about two weeks before the event, and they offered me a writer to help me craft the introduction and presentation speech. I figured this would make it easier, so I took their advice. I didn't want to screw it up with an underwhelming speech. It was too important to me.

I recall receiving the first draft and being unsettled after I went through it. It was nicely stated, but it did not sound like me. Sure, the accolades and compliments and jokes were layered in there fine. But it lacked the heart, humor, and soulful magic that I wanted and needed to share. I wanted the audience to understand my relationship with Pat on a deeper level. Even more, I wanted Pat to hear *my* voice. It was only a few days shy of the live event. I had little to no speech-writing experience, but I told the producers that I was going to submit an alternate version to them within twenty-four hours. And I did. They loved it. It was very emotional and funny and respectful. That was my goal. I had been given the opportunity to say everything I would ever want to say to my acting partner and good friend, and I seized the moment this time.

And it was perfect. The star-studded crowd was predominately made up of the Asian American arts community and the New York City elite. It was a special night for Pat, and I was dialed in and laser-focused in my delivery. It truly played like music at Lincoln Center. Following my speech and clip presentation, the moment in which I introduced him was one I will never forget. He appeared at the opposite end of the stage in his tuxedo and took the long walk across to me at the podium. The formally dressed crowd sprung to their feet with a roar that seemed to last for five minutes. Pat and I hugged, and he said thank you with his signature "I love ya ass, baby." We stood together and took in the echoing applause. Camera flashes strobed throughout the theater, from the first row of the orchestra to the farthest reaches of the balcony. The moment played, suspended in time. It was a gift to everyone in the theater, none more than myself.

Backstage at the event, it was an infusion of laughs and jokes and reminiscences of yesteryear. There were a lot of hugs and kisses and high fives. A few tears, a couple of fart jokes and vintage one-liners. It encompassed our dynamic, and I was thankful that I was there to embrace it with him. Pat passed away one year later, almost to the day. I am so grateful I had that moment to shine in his eyes. I know he's shining down on me now, watching the success of *Cobra Kai*.

The legacy lives on. . . .

CHAPTER TWELVE

Waxing Onward

It was a scheduled noon flight from New York to Los Angeles in February 2017. My plane was delayed—I would be cutting it close. I'd pick up three hours in the air, but I was concerned the delay would still prove to be a problem for my plans. I was attending an important screening at the Santa Barbara International Film Festival that evening. Once I landed, I needed to rent a car at LAX and take the approximately ninety-minute drive up the coast. Now I'd land during rush hour, and I didn't know if the drive would turn into two hours or more. When I got in the car, I was running roughly an hour behind. Fortunately, I made up some time thanks to today's navigation apps. With no chance to shower, I dropped my bags at the hotel, threw on a sports jacket, and quickly splashed some water on my face. From there, I bolted to the theater. Jogging up the street, I ran my fingers through my hair, hoping for the best. At this point I was about thirty minutes late. For someone who prides himself on his punctuality, this was frustrating. I kept telling myself that these things rarely start on time in an attempt to alleviate my tardiness concerns. Anxiously, I hopped up the steps to the theater. I had butterflies, as I hadn't seen the guest of honor in quite some time. The film I was there to see was a documentary feature titled *John G. Avildsen: King of the Underdogs*.

Upon arrival, I noticed the festival's step-and-repeat line was dwindling and the guests were taking their seats inside. I hurriedly skidded into the back of the theater, catching my breath. My eyes were darting around, attempting to find a familiar face, when from the front of the house I heard a voice bellowing, as if he were holding his director's bullhorn, "Oh, boy, look who's here. Wow, it seems they'd let *anyone* into this place!" The audience turned their attention toward me as I stood in the back of the auditorium. Upon recognizing me, they began to laugh. As did I. My nerves were instantly settled. Laughter, always the great icebreaker. I smiled big as I locked eyes with Avildsen. We walked toward each other in the center aisle and met for a warm embrace. It had probably been about three years since I saw him last. His hair looked whiter than before and he was bit frailer than he had been the last time, but his quick-wittedness was up front and center. I noticed Tamlyn Tomita was there, and I was comforted by her being in attendance as well. We all settled into our seats as the filmmaker, Derek Wayne Johnson, introduced John and the film. It was a lovely evening. A celebration of the work of a man who was instrumental in changing my life.

After the screening's Q and A was over, as the theatergoers

were milling around outside, John approached me with a white envelope. It was a basic letter-sized envelope, sealed. Handwritten on the outside in red ink was "For Ralph." Without any fanfare he plainly said, "Hey, before I forget, I brought this if you want." I had no idea what it was, and it was so random. I opened the envelope to find two thirty-five-millimeter film strips about fourteen inches in length folded at their splice point. I held them up to a shaft of light coming from a streetlamp to make out the images. Four scenes with eight to ten frames each had been connected to create the two individual strips. They included images of Miyagi's house. The yellow 1947 Ford convertible. Me in a powder-blue, ruffle-shirted tuxedo and Pat in his Miyagi khakis, from an early sequence in *The Karate Kid Part II*. I don't believe there was any specific rhyme or reason or significance to his choosing these particular pieces of film. I think John just had them somewhere in his house and decided to take them with him once he heard I was attending that night. I thanked him for bringing them and we shared the nostalgia-soaked moment for a brief bit. I carefully placed them back in the envelope, making sure I didn't kink the film before I resealed it. I slid it into my jacket's inside breast pocket, where it remained for the rest of the evening. John did not stay at the event too long after that. He had a car service take him back home to Los Angeles about midway through the small after-party. I, on the other hand, was spending the night in Santa Barbara before driving back down to LA the following morning. We found each other before he took off for the night. I gave him a brief hug and a congratulations on the documentary. We were equally grateful to have been there together, and we shared those sentiments. That was the last moment I spent with John before he passed.

I remember taking the film strips out that night when I was alone in my hotel room in the wee hours. It brought me back to the time when those images had been captured. The pictures were nostalgic, but so was the touch and feel of the celluloid in my hand. To hold this piece of film from yesteryear was so wonderfully bittersweet, an experience that's pretty much gone in today's digital world. I even used my iPhone flashlight to project the images onto the hotel room's ceiling as I lay in bed. Not the clearest picture, but it still looked so cool having the movie frames projected up there.

As I mentioned, this was in early February 2017. John G. Avildsen passed way from pancreatic cancer in June of that same year. I never knew he was sick. I don't believe he shared it with anyone but his immediate family. All of us in the *Karate Kid* family were surprised by the news. Me, Robert, Billy, Marty—we all found out after the fact. John was that type of filmmaker. The camera always pointed forward. He never turned it on himself. He died just a few months before the *Cobra Kai* series concept was officially announced. I don't think he ever knew about the project. And of course, neither did Pat, or Jerry Weintraub, for that matter. Three of the giants who birthed this franchise never got the chance to see and share in the chapter that is currently unfolding. But I know they would not be surprised. They all knew how fertile the ground had become for more story with these characters. We'd even spoken about it at different times. Our thoughts, however, never gained the traction to generate anything specific. It was not meant to be. And then Jon, Josh, and Hayden came forward as the blessed farmers who planted the perfect seed. A spectacular resurgence and outpouring of love from generations old and new is happening right now . . . again. Kamen has expressed to me in multiple emails, "My only regret is that John and Pat didn't get to see this and revel in it as we get to do." I share that sentiment. Make no mistake, I wish they were here to witness this present groundswell. Though I choose to take solace in believing they are beaming in drunken happiness, toasting with the finest of sake from the heavens! That is how I carry it forward in my mind.

Today, I walk the same streets where grade school kids used to ask, "Hey, aren't you the Karate Kid?!" Now it's replaced with, "Hey, don't you play the dad on my favorite show, *Cobra Kai*?!" To which I respond with a wistful chuckle, "Yeah, that's me, I play the dad on your favorite show, *Cobra Kai*." It's fascinating to observe the younger generation backing themselves into the *Karate Kid* film franchise after first discovering *Cobra Kai*. They'll tell me about their moms and dads and how they all watch it together. I'll ask them who their favorite characters are. They will debate with each other, calling out:

"Hawk! He's awesome."
"No way, Miguel is the best!"
"Sam LaRusso!"
"Robby's so cool!"
"Demetri, he's funny."
"Tory is badass."

They root for their own generation of Karate Kids. And they are so passionate. As passionate as fans of this cinematic universe have always been. Our conversation may then segue over to Daniel and Johnny. Some feel Daniel LaRusso is a good guy and others, not so much. It has been the design of *Cobra Kai* to blur those lines. To frame those rivalries in the gray. To at first shine a more sympathetic light onto Johnny Lawrence, thereby setting up LaRusso as less likable. Less of the clear hero that he once was. This was the case certainly at the outset of the show. And then it goes back and forth with all of the show's rivalries, where allegiances may change based on characters' actions. Theoretically, there's a little good and a little bad in everyone. The line between the two becomes distorted, with both Daniel and Johnny having good intentions. That complexity evolves even further as the series grows. I have learned something about storytelling through this experience. The shifting of viewpoints supports the ongoing story and sustains a longer narrative. It has been a clever writing plan by the creative team.

Having walked in the shoes of this character for thirty-four years from one perspective and then altering it to fit the *Cobra Kai* construct was an adjustment. At times it would be challenging for me, and at other times it would give birth to a far more compelling story in the series, even if it wasn't a direction I would have chosen or expected. The road I've traveled has been extraordinary, eye-opening, thought-provoking, and rich. What more can you ask for in a continuation of the *Karate Kid* saga? Though, I will still push and occasionally pull when I feel the need to protect LaRusso in the story. It's a valued part of the respectful collaboration I share with Jon, Josh, and Hayden. Daniel LaRusso is precious to me, and they know that. He's worth it.

It's rare to have an opportunity to go back decades later and build upon a character that is such a part of oneself. To once again wear the white *gi* and place that *hachimaki* back where we remember it, on Daniel LaRusso's forehead, thirty-something years from the last time we saw it there. That moment and sequence from *Cobra Kai*'s episode 5 was a highlight filled with so many nostalgic emotions. I performed the same kata movements that I'd demonstrated in the movie franchise, Bill Conti's music from the original film underscoring the iconic reveal of the Karate Kid today, as a grown man. An emotional high point for me and LaRusso in our freshman season of the show.

I recall the bittersweetness I felt in season 2 when I played the mentor figure to the student, Robby, in Miyagi's backyard. The scene was a montage demonstrating the techniques of waxing, sanding, and painting. Right before rehearsing, I stopped a moment in reflection. I looked around and thought, *This is where all the magic happened in '83*, remembering those scenes with Pat and me in Miyagi's yard. I was overcome and needed to take a moment to collect myself before filming this current version for *Cobra Kai*. I looked at Tanner (Robby), the "kid" standing in what had once been my shoes. With Pat and John and Jerry no longer with me. It was our legacy that I needed to carry on to the next generation with a fresh new story crafted by Jon, Josh, and Hayden. A true passing of the torch. I took a cleansing breath and marched forward as we began to define a new version of those iconic moments for today's audience. And it became their own—familiar, but their own, with an homage to its source.

The Karate Kid's good fortune and success are as evident now as they were then. The franchise continues to be kissed by luck, never ceasing to amaze. The explosion of *Cobra Kai* on Netflix, launching during a global pandemic, may have been just what the fans needed, turns out. It became the ultimate comfort food and warm embrace around a world in need of the joy that it brings. And that joy has been amplified for me in the relationships I have made in the present and the enhancement of those relationships from my past. This resurgence has lifted lifelong friendships to all-new levels. To share in this amazement with my co-star William Zabka after all of these years has been a most wondrous journey. Paying tribute to Pat Morita for a whole new generation has been blissfully rewarding. To reconnect with Robert Kamen, who created the foundation of this world and serves as both an official and unofficial consultant to the *Cobra Kai* team, and reinvigorate our playful dynamic—getting to taste it all again has been beyond delicious. Almost as delicious as the phenomenal cabernet sauvignon he produces from his Sonoma vineyard these days. The enjoyment of tangling once again with Martin Kove, trading blows in front of the camera with his John Kreese, is another piece of candy I never thought I'd get to chew on again. And writing a new chapter alongside Elisabeth Shue was something I never believed would ever happen. I am thrilled that it did. It means more to me than I could have imagined.

I was recently on a recorded Zoom call with Tamlyn Tomita where Sony Pictures was capturing our audio commentary for *The Karate Kid Part II*. This was for their upcoming 4K Ultra HD release of the original *Karate Kid* trilogy. We realized about halfway through, as we were reminiscing about the filmmaking experience, that we had never watched the film together. This was the first and only time. And we both got quiet, lost in nostalgia, while we viewed our younger selves during the beautifully photographed tea-ceremony scene. We watched in silence and let the scene play. Collectively, on opposite ends of the country, we cherished that youthful moment in time that would live forever on film. It was pure. It was innocent. It was honest work. I enjoyed that opportunity after all of these years. I'm not sure it would have presented itself had *Cobra Kai* not blown up on Netflix. And that was sweet to share with her. During the playback of the film, I recognized one of the background players who was also my camera stand-in, Stan Rodarte. He has grown to be one of my best and closest friends to this very day. I soaked in the memories and impact that these films have had on my life from so many vantage points. And I thought of what is to come. . . .

As I headed off to film *Cobra Kai* season 5, I was excited to see my friends. The cast and crew who have become an extended family. To reconnect with Mary Mouser and Griffin Santopietro, who play my kids in the show, and to expand on their stories. To witness the climb of our other young breakout stars, like Xolo and Tanner. And laugh out loud with the instinctively hilarious Courtney Henggeler as we tackle being fake-married for another season, with our friendship and on-screen couple-ness continuing to grow. To watch the evolution of Peyton List's Tory or the rise of Dallas Dupree Young's Kenny, and the comedic timing of Gianni DeCenzo's Demetri. Or the hypertalented Jacob Bertrand, who has become a fan favorite with his turn as Eli/Hawk. And to enter the next chapter with the OG vets, Kove, Yuji, and Thomas Ian Griffith, among others. And of course, to continue peeling back the layers of Daniel and Johnny with my partner in rivalry, Mr. Zabka. A match made in streaming heaven. I look forward to those epic steak dinners that have become a tradition with the core five: Jon, Josh, Hayden, Billy, and myself. Saluting the success as we toast with our ice-ice-cold martinis and sip Robert's highest-level Kamen Estate cab. We are all so grateful to be on this incredible journey.

So now the barrage of questions becomes, where and when will *Cobra Kai* finally land? How many more seasons will it sustain on Netflix? And when it's complete, will there be other stories to explore? Where do we go and how do we get there? A spin-off of the next-generation cast? A prequel of the OG Cobras from the early eighties? Or a Miyagi origin story, which I would personally love to see happen? *Cobra Kai* has opened up the landscape and stretched it wider, with many avenues for development and growth. Perhaps on a smaller scale, the *Karate Kid* franchise is similar to the Marvel Cinematic Universe or *Star Wars*. What perspective or prism may be next to expand upon? There is great opportunity here to continue to scale this mountain in storytelling. The success of *Cobra Kai* has opened the door for that. It will be exciting to see what is next.

But one fact is undeniable. It all traces back to where it began. The summer of 1984. When a kid from Newark met a man from Okinawa in the San Fernando Valley and something wonderful and magical occurred, capturing the hearts and minds of the world. It rolled like thunder decade to decade, building an even wider fan base around the world. There's a well-known phrase I have been hearing more and more in recent days:

Everything old is new again.

I understand why one might say that in this case. And more pointedly, why I hear it directed at me specifically in regard to LaRusso and this franchise. But I see it differently, from where I sit and where I have been. It was never old. It was always present. It never went away. The fans would not allow it to age. They have held on to it and carry it as an affectionate piece of their lives.

The Karate Kid and all of its gifts belong to you, the fans. It is you who have created the longevity. And I pay tribute to each and every one of you, without whom I would not have this book to write. You continue to uphold this legacy and share it with future generations. And I am eager to see where you take it next as it continues to endure and climb to new heights.

Buzz Lightyear once said, "To infinity and beyond!"

Thank you for launching Daniel LaRusso into the stratosphere.

A humble and sincere thank-you, from . . .

. . . *the kid who got the part.*

ACKNOWLEDGMENTS

I'll simply start at the beginning. I am grateful to my parents, Ralph Sr. and Rosalie, who have blessed me with their values and encouragement wherever I venture in my life. My love and gratitude to both of them, as well as to my brother, Steven, for providing me with the foundation of who I am today.

My deepest thanks and appreciation to Robert Mark Kamen for this gift of Daniel (Webber) LaRusso. His creation of this character and franchise has enriched my life beyond words. I treasure our playful banter as we watch the story continue to unfold as we reach our golden years.

To that point, a huge thank-you with admiration to Josh Heald, Jon Hurwitz, and Hayden Schlossberg for the clever formation and global explosion of the *Cobra Kai* series. It has broadened the growth of the *Karate Kid* universe with each and every season.

Special recognition goes out to William Zabka and all of my castmates from *The Karate Kid* films and the *Cobra Kai* series. They have lifted me to heights I never could have imagined and have provided a sustained gust that allows me this flight of a lifetime.

Thanks to the late Jerry Weintraub for being the last of a breed and the man who "put the kid in the picture." Thank you to my friends, past and present, at Columbia Pictures and Sony Pictures Television as well.

My heartfelt gratitude to the late John G. Avildsen and Noriyuki "Pat" Morita (my guiding lights); I am still learning from both of them today. And to the countless storytellers I have had the pleasure to gain experience and grow through: Francis Ford Coppola, Walter Hill, and Todd Holland, to name a few.

Creating this book required a substantial amount of direction for this first-timer, and I am grateful to have had an extraordinary team to support me throughout this new venture. Thank you to my literary agent, Matthew Elblonk, for being the vital sounding board I needed and walking me through the early stages of creating a proposal that ignited such interest within the industry.

I owe an abundance of thanks to my fabulous editor, Jill Schwartzman, at Dutton. An attentive listener who with a guiding hand became my ultimate cheerleader. Thank you for being true to your word of allowing me to write the best version of the book we all set out to create. Thanks to everyone else at Dutton, too, especially Christine Ball, John Parsley, Emily Canders, Katie Taylor, Tiffani Ren, Christopher Lin,

Vi-An Nguyen, LeeAnn Pemberton, Kristin del Rosario, and Marya Pasciuto.

Thank you, Jason Weinberg, Stephanie Simon, Jennifer Merlino, Julia Buchwald, Jonathan Mason, and Tony Burton, for your long-term loyalty and guidance. Additionally, thanks to Tom Hansen, who was there at the start, and Don Steele, who carries that ball today.

When it comes to public relations, for me, there is a choice of only one. My deep appreciation to my publicist, Jill Fritzo. Also to Stephen Fertelmes, Michael Geiser, Charlie Roina, and the rest of her team.

I've heard many say, "You are who your friends are," and if that is the case, I have been blessed with *the best around*. . . . A special thank-you to Stan Rodarte and William LiPera for being the truest of blue to both me and my family. Similarly, I must acknowledge my wife's family for being a constant source of love and support from the earliest days of our courtship.

And, finally, thanks to the three heroes in my life. Thank you, Julia and Daniel, for your patience as I orbited around these stories and for cheering me on to victory every step of the way. Sharing these memories with you is everything. And lastly, to my best friend, my wife, Phyllis, who simultaneously elevates and grounds me. My deepest love, respect, and gratitude for all that is us.

ABOUT THE AUTHOR

An actor, producer, and director with an extensive list of credits, **Ralph Macchio** is best known for his celebrated performance as Johnny in Francis Ford Coppola's *The Outsiders*; the hit film *My Cousin Vinny*; and most notably the title role in the popular classic *The Karate Kid* and its successors. Expanding further on the *Karate Kid* universe, Ralph continues to reprise his iconic role of Daniel LaRusso in the hit Netflix series *Cobra Kai*. He lives on Long Island with his family.